11+

Success

CEM Tests

Practice Test Papers

Book 1

4 test papers,
plus audio download

In partnership with

Philip McMahon

Contents

Guidance notes for parents

What your child will need to sit these papers

- A quiet place to sit the exam
- A clock which is visible to your child
- A way to play the audio download
- A pencil and an eraser
- A piece of paper

Your child should not use a calculator for any of these papers.

How to invigilate the test papers

Your child should sit Test A, Paper 1 then have a 15-minute break. They should then sit Paper 2. Don't help your child or allow any talking. Review the answers with your child and help improve their weaker areas. At a later date, your child should sit Test B, Papers 1 and 2 in a two-hour session.

Step 1: Cut out the answers and keep them hidden from your child.

Step 2: Tear out the answer sheet section. Your child should write their full name on top of the first answer sheet. Give them the question paper booklet. They must not open the paper until they are told to do so by the audio instructions.

Step 3: Start the audio.

Step 4: Ask your child to work through the practice questions before the time starts for each section. An example is already marked on each section of the answer sheet. Your child should mark the answer sheet clearly and check that the practice questions are correctly marked.

Step 5: Mark the answer sheet. Then, together with your child, work through the questions that were answered incorrectly. When working through the Non-verbal Reasoning sections, ensure you have the question papers open to help explain the answers to your child.

How your child should complete the answer sheet

Your child MUST NOT write their answers on the question paper, they must use the answer sheet. They should put a horizontal line through the boxes on the answer sheet. To change an answer, your child should fully erase the incorrect answer and then clearly select a new answer. Any rough workings should be done on a separate piece of paper.

The audio instructions

Both papers have audio instructions to allow your child to learn, listen and act upon audio instructions.

Audio instructions are at the start, during and at the end of the sections. Audio warnings on the time remaining will be given at varying intervals. Your child should listen out for these warnings.

The symbols at the foot of the page

Written instructions are at the foot of the page. Your child MUST follow these instructions:

Continue working

Stop and wait for instructions

Your child can review questions within the allocated time, but must not move onto the next section until they are allowed to do so.

The instructions and examples at the beginning of the section

In the instructions, your child should look for: the time allowed; how many questions there are; and how to complete the answers.

Examples are at the beginning of every section to show the type of question included in a particular section. The example questions will be worked through as part of the audio instructions.

Developing time-management skills and working at speed

These test papers have been used with previous pupils of the CEM exam in various counties. They provide essential practice of the types of questions which could arise, in addition to the strictly timed conditions, which will help your child practise their time-management skills.

Marking the papers

Each question is worth one mark.

Scores

Overall scores your child should be aiming for:

- 75% or more on the first pack of 2 papers if taken in the weeks leading up to the exam
- 70% or more on the second pack of 2 papers if taken in the weeks leading up to the exam.

A weighted score attaches a certain amount of weight to each section in the exam.

How to work out your child's score:

Add together the scores for Non-verbal Reasoning and Maths sections (both Numeracy and Problem Solving). This will give you score A. This relates to both sections in all papers.

Then add together the remaining scores for all English sections, which will give you score B.

Then add scores A and B together and divide them by 2.

This will give you an average weighted score across the 2 packs.

To calculate your child's weighted score as a percentage, divide your child's score by the maximum score, and multiply it by 100.

Once you have completed this, you will have two percentages and the combined weighted score across the two papers is the middle of these two percentages.

For example: If your child scores 46 out of 92 for English, this equals 50%.

If your child scores 62 out of 82, this equals approximately 76%. So the combined weighted score across the two papers is 50% + 76%, which equals 126%. If you divide this by 2, this equals 63%. This is your child's weighted score.

The maximum scores:

Test A Paper 1 English – 49

Test A Paper 1 Maths and Non-verbal Reasoning – 36

Test A Paper 2 English – 43

Test A Paper 2 Maths and Non-verbal Reasoning – 43

Test B Paper 1 English – 48

Test B Paper 1 Maths and Non-verbal Reasoning – 37

Test B Paper 2 English – 35

Test B Paper 2 Maths and Non-verbal Reasoning – 41

English maximum scores, Test A Papers 1 and 2 – 92

Maths and Non-verbal Reasoning maximum scores, Test A Papers 1 and 2 – 79

English maximum scores, Test B Papers 1 and 2 – 83

Maths and Non-verbal Reasoning maximum scores, Test B Papers 1 and 2 – 78

Please note the following:

As the content varies from year to year in CEM exams, a good score in this paper does not guarantee a pass, and a lower score may not always suggest a fail!

What happens if your child does not score a good mark?

Identify strengths and weaknesses

Continue to provide a wide variety of questions to build your child's knowledge. Focus on the areas in which your child did not perform as well.

Timings

Allow your child to continue practising working under timed conditions.

Test A Paper 1

Instructions

1. Ensure you have pencils and an eraser with you.
2. Make sure you are able to see a clock or watch.
3. Write your name on the answer sheet.
4. Do not open the question booklet until you are told to do so by the audio instructions.
5. Listen carefully to the audio instructions given.
6. Mark your answers on the answer sheet only.
7. All workings must be completed on a separate piece of paper.
8. You should not use a calculator, dictionary or thesaurus at any point in this paper.
9. Move through the papers as quickly as possible and with care.
10. Follow the instructions at the foot of each page.
11. You should mark your answers with a horizontal strike, as shown on the answer sheet.
12. If you want to change your answer, ensure that you rub out your first answer and that your second answer is clearly more visible.
13. You can go back and review any questions that are within the section you are working on only. You must await further instructions before moving onto another section.

Symbols and Phrases used in the Tests

Comprehension

 YOU HAVE 9 MINUTES TO COMPLETE THE FOLLOWING SECTION.

YOU HAVE 10 QUESTIONS TO COMPLETE WITHIN THE TIME GIVEN.

EXAMPLES

Comprehension Example

Some people choose to start their Christmas shopping early in October. It has been reported that some people even buy their Christmas presents in the sales in August. In recent years, people have had the option of purchasing their Christmas presents online.

Example 1

According to the passage, what is the earliest that people start their Christmas shopping?

A   In the preceding summer
B   In the preceding October
C   In the preceding November
D   Christmas Eve
E   In early December

The correct answer is A. This has already been marked in Example 1 in the Comprehension section of your answer sheet.

Practice Question 1

In recent years, what has caused a change in how people shop?

A   There are more shops.
B   Shops are more crowded.
C   You can easily organise your journey to the shops.
D   New products are available.
E   There has been a rise in use of the Internet.

The correct answer is E. Please mark this in Practice Question 1 in the Comprehension section of your answer sheet.

STOP AND WAIT FOR FURTHER INSTRUCTIONS

Read the following passage and then answer the questions below.

The History of Art

Art has always been part of society. Even as far back as prehistoric times, early modern humans (Homo sapiens) were expressing their thoughts, beliefs and feelings by producing cave art. There are many examples of Palaeolithic cave art. The finest known example can be found in a cave in Lascaux, in South West France. The vast network of caves is believed to be just under 18,000 years old. The drawings and paintings mainly include the animals which lived in the area at that time. Human figures and other abstract images are also depicted. Visitors are now unable to see the real examples, as the cave is closed to allow the cave art to be preserved. Since 2001, visitors have only been able to visit a replica of the caves.

Other civilisations have expressed their art in different mediums. We have many fragmented examples of hand-crafted sculptures from the Ancient Greeks, Romans and Egyptians. These civilisations also expressed themselves through their monumental architecture. Their public buildings were built on a huge scale and were originally beautifully embellished. Much of this embellishment has now vanished. However, the beauty of these buildings can still be seen, both in the design of the building, and in some small remaining fragments of the decoration.

Much later during the Renaissance period, a new artistic movement, originating in Italy, swept through Western Europe. One characteristic of this movement was the introduction of perspective into works of art. However, the key feature of this new style was 'chiaroscuro', which means 'light' and 'dark'. This gave new emphasis to the illusion of three-dimensional figures, in contrast to the two-dimensional figures that had preceded this period. Figures were more realistic, making them almost lifelike.

Art attracts the interest of communities and individuals. Many wealthy individuals have extensive art collections, which are an expression of their passion for art. Many also buy art as an investment, in the hope that the value of their purchase will rise.

Over the past 30 years, there has been a gradual realisation that art can be beneficial to the community as a whole. In some cases, redevelopment projects now include a piece of 'public art'. This is often a large sculpture, sited in a prominent position to enhance the environment.

Modern art attracts much controversy. Some hold the view that the art of the 21st century should not be viewed as art. Many commentators say that the installations are merely there to attract the attention of the media. Many sculptures are also considered grotesque and in bad taste. However, many of the most successful artists over the centuries have been those who pushed the boundaries, and who initially attracted controversy.

(1) How old is the cave at Lascaux?

    A   Less than 10,000 years old
    B   Over 20,000 years old
    C   Less than 20,000 years old
    D   More than 30,000 years old
    E   Less than 8,000 years old

CONTINUE WORKING

(2) Which phrase best describes the art at Lascaux?

A   Many sculptures of human figures are found at the site
B   There are no paintings of animals
C   The vast majority are paintings of caves
D   There are many sculptures of animals
E   The vast majority of the paintings are of animals

(3) Why are the caves now closed to the public?

A   To allow the caves to be preserved
B   To allow for more visitors to attend
C   To allow for restoration of the area
D   To allow for more time to visit the caves
E   To allow for more replicas to be made

(4) What evidence remains of the art from the ancient civilisations of Rome, Egypt and Greece?

A   Decorations from small sculptures
B   Small buildings and paintings
C   Large sculptures only
D   Fragments of sculptures and large buildings
E   Beautifully embellished clothing

(5) Where did the Renaissance start?

A   In Italy
B   In Rome
C   In England
D   In Egypt
E   In Eastern Europe

(6) Why did the Renaissance have such an impact on painting techniques?

A   Paintings emphasised two-dimensional figures
B   Paintings looked more realistic
C   Portraits of people were no longer painted
D   Paintings were now only produced in colour
E   Paintings were only produced in black and white

CONTINUE WORKING

7 Which of the following is given in the passage as a reason for individuals buying art?

A To give a piece of art to a community
B To help the artist
C To be controversial
D To place it in their garden
E To make an investment

8 What is 'public art'?

A Art placed in a person's house
B Art placed in an area to benefit a community, or newly developed area
C Art created in the 20th century
D Art creating media attention
E Art created to be controversial

9 What is the meaning of the word 'prominent' in the context of the passage?

A Realistic
B Worthwhile
C Egotistical
D Hidden
E Noticeable

10 Which is the phrase that best summarises the final paragraph?

A Modern art is always liked by people
B Modern art is only produced to be installed near the boundaries of communities
C Modern art is traditional
D Modern art is often controversial
E Modern art makes artists wealthy

STOP AND WAIT FOR FURTHER INSTRUCTIONS

Shuffled Sentences

INSTRUCTIONS

 YOU HAVE 8 MINUTES TO COMPLETE THE FOLLOWING SECTION.

YOU HAVE 15 QUESTIONS TO COMPLETE WITHIN THE TIME GIVEN.

EXAMPLES

Example 1

The following sentence is shuffled and also contains one unnecessary word.
Rearrange the sentence correctly in order to identify the unnecessary word.

dog the ran fetch the to stick gluing.

A	B	C	D	E
gluing	dog	ran	the	stick

The correct answer is A. This has already been marked in Example 1 in the Shuffled Sentences section of your answer sheet.

Practice Question 1

The following sentence is shuffled and also contains one unnecessary word.
Rearrange the sentence correctly in order to identify the unnecessary word.

pushed Emma stood up and closed the table under the chairs.

A	B	C	D	E
chairs	stood	under	closed	Emma

The correct answer is D. Please mark this in Practice Question 1 in the Shuffled Sentences section of your answer sheet.

STOP AND WAIT FOR FURTHER INSTRUCTIONS

Each sentence below is shuffled and also contains one unnecessary word.
Rearrange each sentence correctly in order to identify the unnecessary word.

(1) book the reserve is I think film better than the.

A	B	C	D	E
I	better	reserve	film	ticket

(2) curtains to paint she drew warmth in the keep the.

A	B	C	D	E
paint	curtains	warmth	to	the

(3) play the firm record number of insurance kept the claims busy.

A	B	C	D	E
play	record	claims	busy	insurance

(4) up the down pillows are more duck comfortable.

A	B	C	D	E
duck	are	up	comfortable	pillows

(5) quick you need dough to question the be to answer.

A	B	C	D	E
answer	need	quick	dough	question

(6) barbecue since the despite went weather the ahead.

A	B	C	D	E
went	despite	weather	ahead	since

(7) was not stable horse the building earthquake the following.

A	B	C	D	E
earthquake	building	following	horse	was

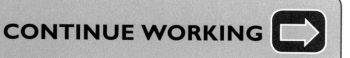

CONTINUE WORKING

8 her up stair to at continued the girl stare.

A	B	C	D	E
stair	continued	girl	her	stare

9 beginning breath she drew a blind before deep her speech.

A	B	C	D	E
before	drew	blind	speech	her

10 tried use the sofa after looking was a years of number tired of.

A	B	C	D	E
sofa	tried	years	use	was

11 the current rain was coming to an end monarch reign the of.

A	B	C	D	E
was	reign	current	monarch	rain

12 kicked small the Roger window through the ball.

A	B	C	D	E
Roger	small	window	ball	through

13 the on the motorway caused in heavy traffic accident.

A	B	C	D	E
on	caused	in	motorway	accident

14 Eva at noon Jon due is to meet earlier.

A	B	C	D	E
earlier	Jon	Eva	noon	at

15 dinner light the rather substantial guests felt bloated after their.

A	B	C	D	E
dinner	the	bloated	light	felt

STOP AND WAIT FOR FURTHER INSTRUCTIONS

Numeracy

INSTRUCTIONS

 YOU HAVE 6 MINUTES TO COMPLETE THE FOLLOWING SECTION.

YOU HAVE 13 QUESTIONS TO COMPLETE WITHIN THE TIME GIVEN.

EXAMPLES

The questions within this section are not multiple choice. Write the answer to each question on the answer sheet by selecting the correct digits from the columns provided.

Example 1

Calculate 14 + 23

The correct answer is 37. This has already been marked in Example 1 in the Numeracy section of your answer sheet.

Practice Question 1

Calculate 83 – 75

The correct answer is 8. Please mark this in Practice Question 1 in the Numeracy section of your answer sheet. Note that a single-digit answer should be marked with a 0 in the left-hand column, so mark 08 on your answer sheet.

STOP AND WAIT FOR FURTHER INSTRUCTIONS

(1) Calculate the answer to the following:

$3 \times 5 - 4$

CONTINUE WORKING

(2) Calculate the answer to the following:

$24 - 4 \div 2$

(3) Calculate the answer to the following:

$18 - 6 \div 3$

(4) Select the appropriate number or numbers to complete the sequence in place of the ?

0, 1, 1, 2, ?, 5, 8

(5) Calculate the range of the following data:

4, 2, 5, 8, 2, 11, 14, 1, 5, 3, 7, 8, 9, 10

(6) Which of these is not exactly divisible by 7?

17, 49, 28, 56, 70

(7) Which of these is not a factor of 63?

1, 19, 21, 63, 3

(8) Which of these is a common factor of both 18 and 48?

4, 24, 12, 6, 7

(9) In three years' time, I will be twice as old as I am now. How old am I now?

(10) Alan was 9, two years ago. How old will he be in one year's time?

(11) How many months are there from 30 April to 30 November?

(12) How many weeks are there in the 9 months from the start of a non-leap year to the end of September?

(13) Calculate what number between 40 and 50 has a remainder of 7 when divided by 9.

STOP AND WAIT FOR FURTHER INSTRUCTIONS ⊗

Problem Solving

 INSTRUCTIONS

 YOU HAVE 8 MINUTES TO COMPLETE THE FOLLOWING SECTION.

YOU HAVE 10 QUESTIONS TO COMPLETE WITHIN THE TIME GIVEN.

EXAMPLES

Example 1

Calculate the following:

If I buy five apples at 20p each and four bananas at 35p each, how much change will I receive if I pay with a £5 note?

A   £2.60
B   £3.40
C   £2.40
D   £3.60
E   £1.35

The correct answer is A. This has already been marked in Example 1 in the Problem Solving section of your answer sheet.

Practice Question 1

Calculate the following: There are 17 people on a bus when it arrives at a bus stop. Eleven people get on the bus, and three get off. How many people are then left on the bus?

A   28
B   31
C   34
D   25
E   14

The correct answer is D. Please mark this in Practice Question 1 in the Problem Solving section of your answer sheet.

STOP AND WAIT FOR FURTHER INSTRUCTIONS

Calculate the following.

(1) If a bag of 50 marbles is shared between friends so that the friends have 10 marbles, 15 marbles and 25 marbles, in what ratio have they been shared?

A   1 : 2   **B**   1 : 2 : 5   **C**   2 : 4 : 8
D   2 : 3 : 5   **E**   10 : 10 : 20

(2) I am unaware that my watch stopped at 7:15 a.m. I check my watch on the way to the station. The correct time then is 7:30 a.m. Thinking I am early, I then buy a cup of coffee taking 10 minutes. My train is due to depart at 7:35 a.m. How late does the train need to be in order for me to catch it?

A   3 minutes   **B**   6 minutes   **C**   2 minutes
D   1 minutes   **E**   4 minutes

Questions 3, 4 and 5 are linked so that questions 4 and 5 follow on from question 3.

(3) A class has 30 children in it. 60% of the children in the class are girls. How many boys are in the class?

A   16   **B**   18   **C**   15
D   14   **E**   12

(4) If five new children join the class at the start of the next year, how many girls are there in the larger class if there are still 60% girls in the larger class?

A   21   **B**   14   **C**   12
D   15   **E**   18

(5) What is the ratio of boys to girls in the larger class in its simplest form?

A   12 : 18   **B**   5 : 3   **C**   10 : 6
D   2 : 3   **E**   21 : 14

(6) There are three buses every hour from Gerrards Cross to Beaconsfield, with buses departing at regular, equally spaced intervals. If the buses are always on time, what is the longest I would have to wait at the bus stop?

A   Just under 20 minutes
B   Just over 20 minutes
C   Just under 5 minutes
D   Just over 5 minutes
E   10 minutes

CONTINUE WORKING ➡

7 What is the average time I would have to wait for a bus if I arrived at the bus stop in Gerrards Cross at random times, during which there were buses every 20 minutes (three buses per hour)?

| A | 20 minutes | B | 6 minutes | C | 10 minutes |
| D | 15 minutes | E | 7 minutes | | |

8 If the bus travels a three-mile journey in 20 minutes, what is its average speed for the journey in mph?

| A | 0 mph | B | 60 mph | C | 30 mph |
| D | 9 mph | E | 3 mph | | |

9 What is the length of time between:

10 past nine in the morning and a quarter to 4 in the afternoon?

A   6 hours 35 minutes
B   5 hours 35 minutes
C   6 hours 25 minutes
D   7 hours 25 minutes
E   8 hours

10 There are 2847 people in a large secondary school. 1527 are girls and teachers. 2649 are girls or boys.

Use the information above to calculate the number of girls, boys and teachers.

A   1450 girls, 1120 boys, 150 teachers
B   1320 girls, 1329 boys, 198 teachers
C   1239 girls, 1230 boys, 198 teachers
D   769 girls, 1820 boys, 168 teachers
E   1329 girls, 1320 boys, 198 teachers

STOP AND WAIT FOR FURTHER INSTRUCTIONS ⊗

Synonyms

INSTRUCTIONS

 YOU HAVE 7 MINUTES TO COMPLETE THE FOLLOWING SECTION.

YOU HAVE 24 QUESTIONS TO COMPLETE WITHIN THE TIME GIVEN.

EXAMPLES

Example 1

Select the word that is most similar in meaning to the following word:

cold

A	B	C	D	E
collect	fence	foggy	windy	chilly

The correct answer is E. This has already been marked in Example 1 in the Synonyms section of your answer sheet.

Practice Question 1

Select the word that is most similar in meaning to the following word:

start

A	B	C	D	E
cramped	begin	free	without	change

The correct answer is B. Please mark this in Practice Question 1 in the Synonyms section of your answer sheet.

STOP AND WAIT FOR FURTHER INSTRUCTIONS

For each row, select the word from the table that is most similar in meaning to the word above the table.

(1) abundance

A	B	C	D	E
jumping	squeeze	exclusion	scarcity	plenty

(2) tranquil

A	B	C	D	E
agitate	calm	pointless	tame	trite

(3) obstinate

A	B	C	D	E
economy	inspiring	inflexible	forgiving	pleasant

(4) erratic

A	B	C	D	E
coy	succinct	affable	volatile	serene

(5) melancholy

A	B	C	D	E
crude	suitable	automatic	multitude	sad

(6) helix

A	B	C	D	E
spiral	rebuke	barbaric	helicopter	submarine

(7) obtuse

A	B	C	D	E
angle	unintelligent	bright	devout	triumphant

(8) adequate

A	B	C	D	E
exercise	unfit	suitable	earthquake	complex

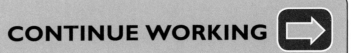

CONTINUE WORKING

9 tenacity

A	B	C	D	E
incite	evade	evaluate	scarcity	resoluteness

10 insolent

A	B	C	D	E
confess	solemn	multitude	rude	solvent

11 enchanted

A	B	C	D	E
delighted	deplorable	egotistic	impertinent	insolent

12 affable

A	B	C	D	E
affected	majestic	resourceful	fallible	amiable

13 contingent

A	B	C	D	E
contain	dependent	subtract	greet	astonish

14 bulging

A	B	C	D	E
injure	flaw	forehead	convex	wound

15 uninterested

A	B	C	D	E
apathetic	intended	overseas	anger	serene

16 box

A	B	C	D	E
din	lucid	advance	crate	distinctive

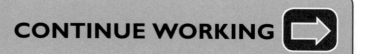

CONTINUE WORKING

17 twisted

A	B	C	D	E
respond	attire	mystify	gnarled	inflexible

18 wound

A	B	C	D	E
flustered	coy	injure	motion	part

19 hopeful

A	B	C	D	E
doctor	berate	optimistic	subsequent	congregate

20 importance

A	B	C	D	E
significance	naïve	distinctive	madness	litter

21 proof

A	B	C	D	E
vital	derivative	evidence	necessary	select

22 adapt

A	B	C	D	E
mimic	homicide	acclimatise	liable	culprit

23 stroll

A	B	C	D	E
bogus	saunter	moreover	icon	velocity

24 copy

A	B	C	D	E
transcribe	dogma	cautious	malevolent	ruffian

STOP AND WAIT FOR FURTHER INSTRUCTIONS ✖

Non-Verbal Reasoning

INSTRUCTIONS

 YOU HAVE 7 MINUTES TO COMPLETE THE FOLLOWING SECTION.

YOU HAVE 13 QUESTIONS TO COMPLETE WITHIN THE TIME GIVEN.

EXAMPLES

REFLECTION Example 1

Select how the following shape or pattern would appear when reflected in the dashed line:

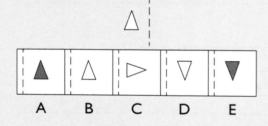

The correct answer is B. This has already been marked in Example 1 in the Non-Verbal Reasoning section of your answer sheet.

REFLECTION Practice Question 1

Select how the following shape or pattern would appear when reflected in the dashed line:

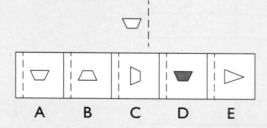

The correct answer is A. Please mark this in Practice Question 1 in the Non-Verbal Reasoning section of your answer sheet.

CONTINUE WORKING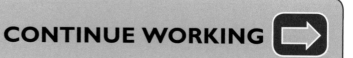

CONNECTION Example 2

Look at the two shapes on the left immediately below. Find the connection between them.

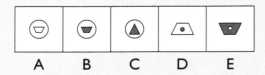

Select the shape that is related to the third shape above by applying the same connection.

The correct answer is B. This has already been marked in Example 2 in the Non-Verbal Reasoning section of your answer sheet.

CONNECTION Practice Question 2

Look at the two shapes on the left immediately below. Find the connection between them.

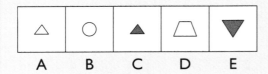

Select the shape that is related to the third shape above by applying the same connection.

The correct answer is E. Please mark this in Practice Question 2 in the Non-Verbal Reasoning section of your answer sheet.

STOP AND WAIT FOR FURTHER INSTRUCTIONS

1 Look at the two shapes on the left immediately below.
Find the connection between them and apply it to the third shape.

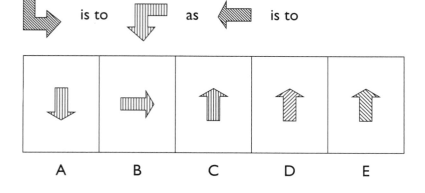

A	B	C	D	E

2 Look at the two shapes on the left immediately below.
Find the connection between them and apply it to the third shape.

A	B	C	D	E

3 Select the correct picture from the row on the right in order to finish the incomplete sequence on the left.

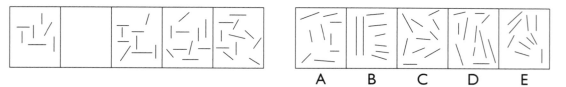

A	B	C	D	E

4 Select the correct picture from the row on the right in order to finish the incomplete sequence on the left.

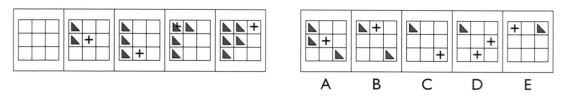

A	B	C	D	E

CONTINUE WORKING

5 Which shape or pattern completes the larger square?

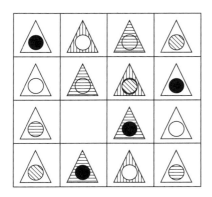

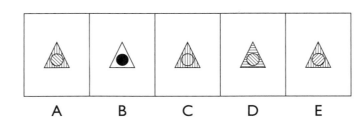

| A | B | C | D | E |

6 Which shape or pattern completes the larger square in the place of the?

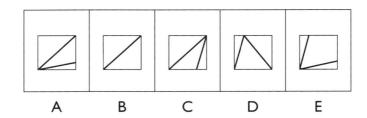

| A | B | C | D | E |

7 Select how the following shape or pattern would appear when reflected in the dashed line.

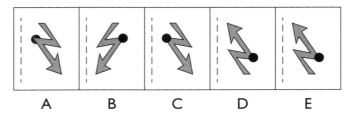

| A | B | C | D | E |

8 Select how the following shape or pattern would appear when reflected in the dashed line.

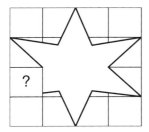

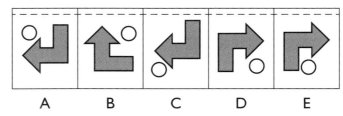

| A | B | C | D | E |

CONTINUE WORKING

9 Select from the five images in the row below, the one image that is a reflection of the image on the left.

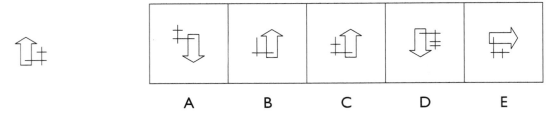

| A | B | C | D | E |

10 Select from the five images in the row below, the one image that is a reflection of the image on the left.

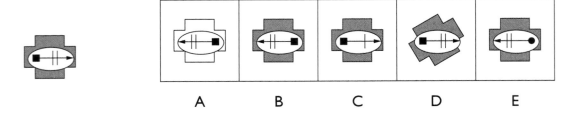

| A | B | C | D | E |

11 Select from the five images in the row below, the one image that is a reflection of the image on the left.

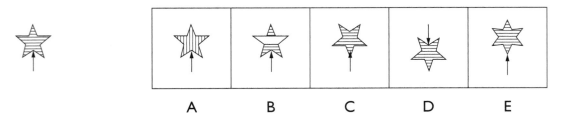

| A | B | C | D | E |

12 Select from the five images in the row below, the one image that is a reflection of the image on the left.

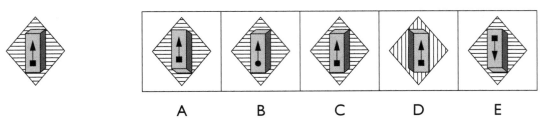

| A | B | C | D | E |

13 Select from the five images in the row below, the one image that is a reflection of the image on the left.

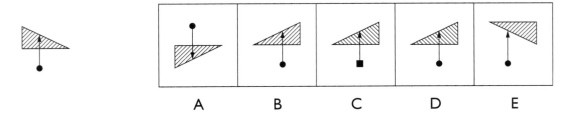

| A | B | C | D | E |

END OF PAPER

Test A Paper 2

Instructions

1. Ensure you have pencils and an eraser with you.
2. Make sure you are able to see a clock or watch.
3. Write your name on the answer sheet.
4. Do not open the question booklet until you are told to do so by the audio instructions.
5. Listen carefully to the audio instructions given.
6. Mark your answers on the answer sheet only.
7. All workings must be completed on a separate piece of paper.
8. You should not use a calculator, dictionary or thesaurus at any point in this paper.
9. Move through the papers as quickly as possible and with care.
10. Follow the instructions at the foot of each page.
11. You should mark your answers with a horizontal strike, as shown on the answer sheet.
12. If you want to change your answer, ensure that you rub out your first answer and that your second answer is clearly more visible.
13. You can go back and review any questions that are within the section you are working on only. You must await further instructions before moving onto another section.

Symbols and Phrases used in the Tests

 Instructions
 Time allowed for this section
 Stop and wait for further instructions
 Continue working

Problem Solving

  INSTRUCTIONS

YOU HAVE 8 MINUTES TO COMPLETE THE FOLLOWING SECTION.

YOU HAVE 10 QUESTIONS TO COMPLETE WITHIN THE TIME GIVEN.

EXAMPLES

A £2.60	B £3.40	C £2.40	D 25	E £1.35
F £3.40	G 14	H 31	I 28	J 34

Example 1

Calculate the following:

If I buy five apples at 20p each, and four bananas at 35p each, how much change will I receive if I pay with a £5 note.

The correct answer is A. This has already been marked in Example 1 in the Problem Solving section of your answer sheet.

Practice Question 1

Calculate the following:

There are 17 people on a bus when it arrives at a bus stop. Eleven people get on the bus, and three get off. How many people are then left on the bus?

The correct answer is D. Please mark this in Practice Question 1 in the Problem Solving section of your answer sheet.

STOP AND WAIT FOR FURTHER INSTRUCTIONS

A 40p	B 20p	C 100	D 45 minutes	E 19,200
F 240	G 50 minutes	H 30p	I £6.80	J £3.20

Several questions will follow for you to answer. Select an answer to each question from the 10 different possible answers in the table above. You may use an answer for more than one question.

(1) Harji is in a supermarket and buys the following:

Four pears at 40p each and twice as many apples, which cost half the price of the pears. How much change should Harji receive if she pays with a £10 note?

(2) Harji also buys the following to make a fruit salad:

Bananas (B) and Kiwis (K)

Use the following information to work out the price in pence of one banana:

4B + 6K = 260 pence

5B + 6K = 280 pence

(3) Harji notices a special offer on yoghurt. The normal price (without the offer) is £1.20 per pot of yoghurt.

The offer is 'Buy 3 for the price of 2'.

How much less would each pot of yoghurt cost under the offer, if three pots are bought?

(4) Harji entered the supermarket at quarter to 11 that morning. She is due to meet her friend for a coffee in the supermarket at half-past 12 in the afternoon. Her shopping in the supermarket takes 55 minutes. How long does Harji have to wait to meet her friend after completing her shopping (her friend arrives five minutes early)?

(5) Harji buys some frozen food as part of her shopping and wants to get home before it defrosts. She places the frozen food in her trolley at 12.20 (5 minutes before she meets her friend). She is with her friend for 15 minutes.

Her drive home is 20 km, and she drives at an average speed of 40 km/h.

When Harji arrives home, how long has the frozen food been out of the freezer?

CONTINUE WORKING

(6) The supermarket serves free coffee to its customers. If the supermarket has served 180 coffees between opening time (8 a.m.) and noon, and for the entire day (until 8 p.m.) there were 420 coffees served, how many coffees were served between noon and closing time?

(7) The dimensions of the supermarket floor are 80 m long by 60 m wide.

The entire floor is covered by square tiles with the following dimensions:

50 cm by 50 cm

How many tiles are required to cover the entire floor area?

(8) If seven lemons cost £1.40, how much do 16 lemons cost?

(9) There are seven women working at the supermarket for every five men. If there are 140 women working at the supermarket, how many men work at the supermarket?

(10) The total cost of the shopping is £123.27. Harji hands over £130 to the man at the checkout. Harji realises that the man on the checkout has not given her enough change when she counts the change of £6.43. How much additional change should Harji have received?

STOP AND WAIT FOR FURTHER INSTRUCTIONS

Cloze

INSTRUCTIONS

 YOU HAVE 10 MINUTES TO COMPLETE THE FOLLOWING SECTION.

YOU HAVE 20 QUESTIONS TO COMPLETE WITHIN THE TIME GIVEN.

EXAMPLES

Example 1

Read the sentence below and select the most appropriate word from the table.

A	B	C	D	E
backdrop	carefully	drawer	disadvantage	dilution

The undulating hills were the perfect Q1 _____ for the watercolour painting.

Please select your answer to go in the place of (Q1) in the above sentence.

The correct answer is A. This has already been marked in Example 1 in the Cloze section of your answer sheet.

Practice Question 1

Read the sentence below and select the most appropriate word from the table.

A	B	C	D	E
had	interior	success	attend	absent

The girl decided she would like to Q2 _____ the party.

Please select your answer to go in the place of (Q2) in the above sentence.

The correct answer is D. Please mark the answer D in Practice Question 1 in the Cloze section of your answer sheet.

STOP AND WAIT FOR FURTHER INSTRUCTIONS

Read the passage and select the most appropriate word from the table below.

A	B	C	D	E
parking	properties	competitive	multitude	aspire

F	G	H	I	J
description	extended	stylish	external	exemplified

The UK Housing Market

Most young people (Q1) _____ to own their own home. Low interest rates have allowed people to afford monthly mortgage payments. However, after a long period of interest rates remaining at an all time low, interest rates are set to rise.

Since the housing market boom of the 1980s, estate agency has been a profitable, but (Q2) _____ marketplace.

Many estate agents now advertise on the Internet, using well-established websites to market their (Q3) _____. A typical house will be advertised with a (Q4) _____ of internal and (Q5) _____ photographs. There is usually a (Q6) _____ of the property, as well as floor plans which show the layout and room sizes. A typical description includes details, such as those (Q7) _____ in the following passage:

'A well proportioned and (Q8) _____ four bedroom end of terrace family house, in a highly sought-after residential area, within easy reach of good local schools and shops. The accommodation has been (Q9) _____ by the current owners and comprises in brief: a storm porch, entrance hall, living room with double doors leading to a dining room, a modern fitted kitchen/breakfast room, an orangery, downstairs cloakroom, four bedrooms, two en-suite shower rooms and a bathroom. Further benefits include gas fired central heating, double glazing, a rear garden laid mostly to lawn and off road (Q10) _____.'

CONTINUE WORKING

Read the passage and select the most appropriate word from the table below.

A	B	C	D	E
empire	ancient	turbulent	theatre	collapsed

F	G	H	I	J
understood	spectators	survive	buildings	Italy

The Origins Of Theatre

In the early 3rd century BC, life in (Q11)_____ Greece changed. Alexander the Great died and his (Q12)_____ fragmented. These became (Q13)_____ times and it was at this time that the (Q14)_____ played a central role in the daily lives of Ancient Greeks.

Theatres could hold tens of thousands of (Q15)_____.

The comedies which were shown, were so popular that they spread to other areas of the ancient world, even as far as (Q16)_____. Comedy is understood by all and is (Q17)_____ by people from all walks of life.

The Romans attacked Greece from 282 BC onwards, and eventually the Greek empire (Q18)_____. The Romans embraced Greek culture and the (Q19)_____ that still (Q20)_____ today in Ancient Rome, allude to the Greek culture that the Romans wanted to replicate.

STOP AND WAIT FOR FURTHER INSTRUCTIONS

Non-Verbal Reasoning

 YOU HAVE 8 MINUTES TO COMPLETE THE FOLLOWING SECTION.

YOU HAVE 15 QUESTIONS TO COMPLETE WITHIN THE TIME GIVEN.

EXAMPLES

CUBES Example 1

Look at the cube net below. Select the only cube that could be formed from the net below.

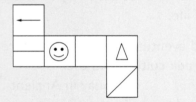 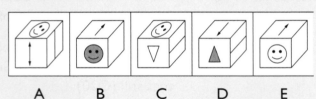

The correct answer is E. This has already been marked in Example 1 in the Non-Verbal Reasoning section of your answer sheet.

CUBES Practice Question 1

Look at the cube net below. Select the only cube that could be formed from the net below.

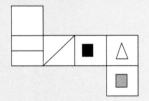 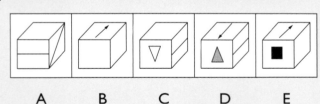

The correct answer is A. Please mark this in Practice Question 1 in the Non-Verbal Reasoning section of your answer sheet.

CONTINUE WORKING ⇨

BELONGS TO GROUP Example 2

Which of the patterns in the row below belongs in the group within the oval?

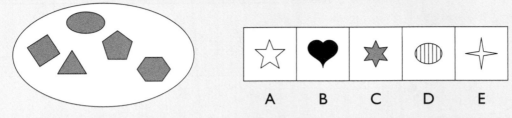

The correct answer is C. This has already been marked in Example 2 in the Non-Verbal Reasoning section of your answer sheet.

BELONGS TO GROUP Practice Question 2

Which of the patterns in the row below belongs in the group within the oval?

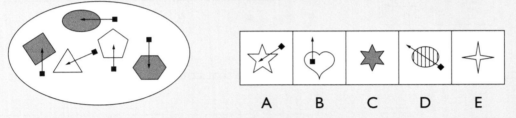

The correct answer is A. Please mark this in Practice Question 2 in the Non-Verbal Reasoning section of your answer sheet.

STOP AND WAIT FOR FURTHER INSTRUCTIONS

(1) Which of the patterns in the row below belongs in the group within the oval?

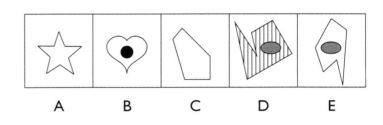

CONTINUE WORKING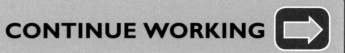

(2) Which of the patterns in the row below belongs in the group within the oval?

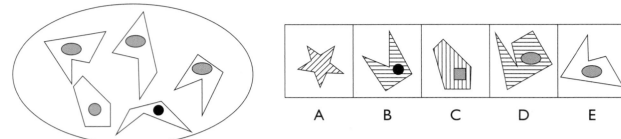

A   B   C   D   E

(3) Which of the patterns in the row below belongs in the group within the oval?

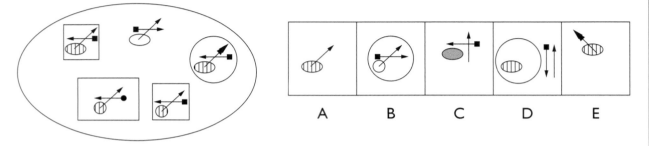

A   B   C   D   E

(4) Look at the cube net below. Select the only cube that could be formed from the net.

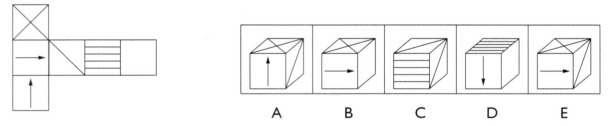

A   B   C   D   E

(5) Look at the cube net below. Select the only cube that could be formed from the net.

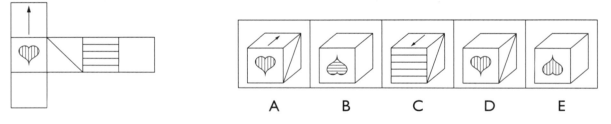

A   B   C   D   E

(6) Look at the cube net below. Select the only cube that could be formed from the net.

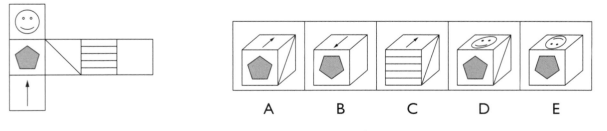

A   B   C   D   E

CONTINUE WORKING ▷

7 Look at the cube net below. Select the only cube that could be formed from the net.

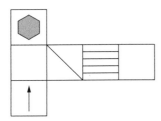

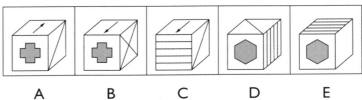

A B C D E

8 Look at the cube net below. Select the only cube that could be formed from the net.

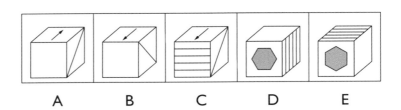

A B C D E

9 Look at the codes for the following patterns and identify the missing code for the pattern on the far right.

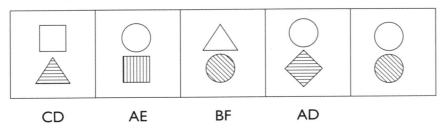

 CD AE BF AD

A	AF
B	AE
C	BD
D	AC
E	CE

10 Look at the codes for the following patterns and identify the missing code for the pattern on the far right.

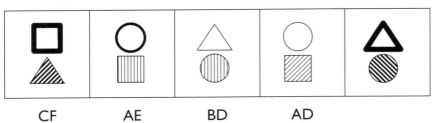

 CF AE BD AD

A	BE
B	AE
C	BD
D	BF
E	CE

11 Look at the codes for the following patterns and identify the missing code for the pattern on the far right.

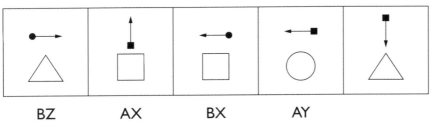

 BZ AX BX AY

A	AX
B	AZ
C	BZ
D	BY
E	BX

CONTINUE WORKING ➡

(12) Look at the codes for the following patterns and identify the missing code for the pattern on the far right.

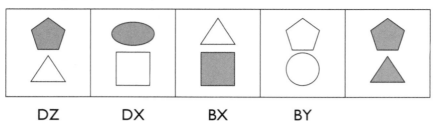

| DZ | DX | BX | BY |

A   DY
B   DX
C   BZ
D   BY
E   DZ

(13) Look at the codes for the following patterns and identify the missing code for the pattern on the far right.

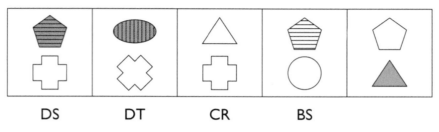

| DS | DT | CR | BS |

A   DR
B   CR
C   BS
D   BT
E   CS

(14) Look at the codes for the following patterns and identify the missing code for the pattern on the far right.

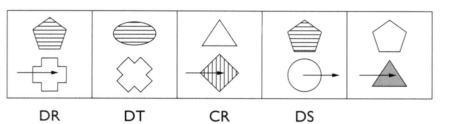

| DR | DT | CR | DS |

A   CR
B   DT
C   CT
D   BT
E   CS

(15) Look at the codes for the following patterns and identify the missing code for the pattern on the far right.

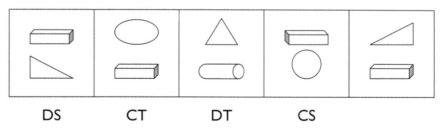

| DS | CT | DT | CS |

A   CT
B   DS
C   DT
D   CS
E   CR

STOP AND WAIT FOR FURTHER INSTRUCTIONS ⊗

Grammar

INSTRUCTIONS

 YOU HAVE 5 MINUTES TO COMPLETE THE FOLLOWING SECTION.

YOU HAVE 8 QUESTIONS TO COMPLETE WITHIN THE TIME GIVEN.

EXAMPLES

Example 1

Select the word below that is misspelt.

A	B	C	D	E
cinema	while	repeet	home	open

The correct answer is C. This has already been marked in Example 1 in the Grammar section of your answer sheet.

Practice Question 1

Select the correct prefix or suffix below to give the opposite to the word 'legal':

A	B	C	D	E
in	im	un	il	non

The correct answer is D. Please mark the answer D in Practice Question 1 in the Grammar section of your answer sheet.

STOP AND WAIT FOR FURTHER INSTRUCTIONS

1 Identify a homophone of the word 'sew' from the words below.

A	B	C	D	E
seen	pig	piglet	sewn	sow

2 Identify the homograph of the word 'bow' from the words below.

A	B	C	D	E
tie	bow	head	royal	boat

3 Select the correct prefix or suffix below to give the opposite to the word 'probable'.

A	B	C	D	E
in	im	dis	un	de

4 Select the word below that is misspelt.

A	B	C	D	E
comittee	whom	once	home	since

5 Select the word below that is misspelt.

A	B	C	D	E
beret	embark	curiousity	apex	appalled

6 Select the word below that is misspelt.

A	B	C	D	E
dilemna	client	burn	bedroom	appalled

7 Select the word below that is misspelt.

A	B	C	D	E
acquire	abate	abstain	adept	existance

8 Select the word below that is misspelt.

A	B	C	D	E
futher	simile	sly	sham	sty

STOP AND WAIT FOR FURTHER INSTRUCTIONS

Antonyms

INSTRUCTIONS

 YOU HAVE 5 MINUTES TO COMPLETE THE FOLLOWING SECTION.

YOU HAVE 15 QUESTIONS TO COMPLETE WITHIN THE TIME GIVEN.

EXAMPLE I

Which word is least similar to the following word:

light

A	B	C	D	E
dark	water	feather	bright	hill

The correct answer is A. This has already been marked in Example 1 in the Antonyms section of your answer sheet.

Practice Question 1

Which word is least similar to the following word:

smooth

A	B	C	D	E
allow	beneath	rough	whilst	shade

The correct answer is C. Please mark the answer C in Practice Question 1 in the Antonyms section of your answer sheet.

STOP AND WAIT FOR FURTHER INSTRUCTIONS

Which word is least similar to the following word:

(1) audible

A	B	C	D	E
inaudible	common	thrive	reaction	unfriendly

(2) immense

A	B	C	D	E
advance	selfish	success	tiny	narrow

(3) just

A	B	C	D	E
simple	hinder	unjust	absurd	disadvantage

(4) condone

A	B	C	D	E
condemn	loose	keep	common	victory

(5) lazy

A	B	C	D	E
free	industrious	unwise	right	frank

(6) essential

A	B	C	D	E
inessential	public	polite	encouraged	disobedient

(7) leader

A	B	C	D	E
lazy	loose	deter	follower	dissuade

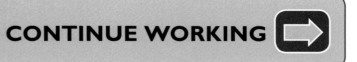

CONTINUE WORKING

8 disdain

A	B	C	D	E
success	failure	admiration	aggressive	awkward

9 prohibit

A	B	C	D	E
allow	valley	victory	dissuade	narrow

10 obedient

A	B	C	D	E
maintain	presence	extract	disobedient	preserve

11 prudent

A	B	C	D	E
imprudent	calm	dense	shallow	encouraged

12 inconspicuous

A	B	C	D	E
maintain	allow	thrive	lever	noticeable

13 wisdom

A	B	C	D	E
clear	silence	folly	maximum	find

14 ominous

A	B	C	D	E
auspicious	fright	repulsive	deceitful	reaction

15 abstain

A	B	C	D	E
frank	immigration	abundant	use	smart

STOP AND WAIT FOR FURTHER INSTRUCTIONS

Numeracy

INSTRUCTIONS

 YOU HAVE 9 MINUTES TO COMPLETE THE FOLLOWING SECTION.

YOU HAVE 18 QUESTIONS TO COMPLETE WITHIN THE TIME GIVEN.

EXAMPLES

The questions within this section are not multiple choice. Write the answer to each question on the answer sheet by selecting the correct digits from the columns provided.

Example 1

Calculate 14 + 23

The correct answer is 37. This has already been marked in Example 1 in the Numeracy section of your answer sheet.

Practice Question 1

Calculate 83 − 75

The correct answer is 8. Please mark the answer in Practice Question 1 in the Numeracy section of your answer sheet. Note that a single-digit answer should be marked with a 0 in the left-hand column. So mark 08 on your answer sheet.

STOP AND WAIT FOR FURTHER INSTRUCTIONS

For the questions in this section that are not multiple choice, you should write the answer to the question on the answer sheet by selecting the digits from the columns of brackets.

(1) How many weeks are there in half of a non-leap year?

CONTINUE WORKING

(2) Calculate $60 + 2 \times 2$

(3) Select the appropriate number or numbers to complete the sequence in place of the ? in the brackets below:

169, 15, 144, 14, 121, ?

(4) Which of these is not divisible by 5?

20, 65, 95, 48, 100

(5) Calculate how many sixths there are in the answer to the following:

$$\frac{2}{3} + \frac{1}{6}$$

(6) If 0.2 were written as a fraction, with the numerator being 1, what would the denominator be?

(7) If 0.585 were rounded to 2 significant figures, the answer would contain how many hundredths?

(8) If 9.95 was rounded to 1 decimal place, and then the answer subtracted from 10, how many tenths would be in the answer?

(9) Which of these is not divisible by 50?

200, 360, 150, 400, 50

| **A** | 200 | **B** | 360 | **C** | 150 |
| **D** | 400 | **E** | 50 | | |

(10) Calculate the radius of the circle below, which has a diameter of 10 cm.

10 cm

| **A** | 10 | **B** | 31.4 | **C** | 3.14 |
| **D** | 25 | **E** | 5 | | |

CONTINUE WORKING ⇨

(11) Calculate the following:

The perimeter of a semi-circle with the straight edge measuring 10 cm.

A	20 cm	**B**	5 cm	**C**	31.4 cm
D	25.7 cm	**E**	15.7 cm		

(12) Calculate the mean value of the following data:

5, 3, 6, 8, 3, 6, 5, 6, 2, 5

A	36	**B**	49	**C**	4.9
D	5	**E**	4		

(13) Select an expression which describes the following:

The remainder of a cake, after 2 people have eaten some. The first person eats twice the amount of cake that the second person eats. The second person eats 1 slice. The cake is cut into 6 equal slices. The size of the whole cake is P. Both people eat all the cake they are served.

A	$\dfrac{3}{8}$	**B**	3	**C**	P
D	0.5P	**E**	3P		

(14) Consider the probability of the following situation:

If I roll a dice and it shows a 3, and then roll a second dice, what is the probability that the total of the dice will be higher than 3?

A	1 in 6	**B**	2 in 6	**C**	4 in 6
D	6 in 6	**E**	3 in 6		

(15) There are two parallel lines of equal length on a graph. The first line has coordinates starting at (0, 3) and ending at (4, 9). The second line starts at coordinates (3, 0). Find the coordinates of the end of the second line, if the second point of each line is the same direction from the first point.

A	(7, 6)	**B**	(6, 7)	**C**	(5, 4)
D	(−7, 6)	**E**	(7, −6)		

CONTINUE WORKING ⇨

(16) Calculate the following:

$$\frac{1}{2} \times \frac{2}{7}$$

A $\quad \frac{1}{7}$ B $\quad \frac{1}{14}$ C $\quad \frac{2}{4}$

D $\quad \frac{14}{2}$ E $\quad \frac{2}{3}$

(17) Calculate the following:

$$\frac{3}{4} \times \frac{8}{12}$$

A $\quad \frac{2}{5}$ B $\quad \frac{1}{3}$ C $\quad \frac{1}{2}$

D $\quad \frac{12}{48}$ E $\quad \frac{11}{16}$

(18) Calculate the following:

$$\frac{3}{9} \div \frac{1}{3}$$

A $\quad 1$ B $\quad \frac{1}{9}$ C $\quad \frac{3}{9}$

D $\quad \frac{4}{12}$ E $\quad \frac{3}{24}$

END OF PAPER

Test B Paper 1

Instructions

1. Ensure you have pencils and an eraser with you.

2. Make sure you are able to see a clock or watch.

3. Write your name on the answer sheet.

4. Do not open the question booklet until you are told to do so by the audio instructions.

5. Listen carefully to the audio instructions given.

6. Mark your answers on the answer sheet only.

7. All workings must be completed on a separate piece of paper.

8. You should not use a calculator, dictionary or thesaurus at any point in this paper.

9. Move through the papers as quickly as possible and with care.

10. Follow the instructions at the foot of each page.

11. You should mark your answers with a horizontal strike, as shown on the answer sheet.

12. If you want to change your answer, ensure that you rub out your first answer and that your second answer is clearly more visible.

13. You can go back and review any questions that are within the section you are working on only. You must await further instructions before moving onto another section.

Symbols and Phrases used in the Tests

 Instructions

 Time allowed for this section

Stop and wait for further instructions

 Continue working

Comprehension

  INSTRUCTIONS

 YOU HAVE 8 MINUTES TO COMPLETE THE FOLLOWING SECTION.

YOU HAVE 10 QUESTIONS TO COMPLETE WITHIN THE TIME GIVEN.

EXAMPLES

Comprehension Example

Some people choose to start their Christmas shopping early in October. It has been reported that some people even buy their Christmas presents in the sales in August. In recent years, people have the option of purchasing their Christmas presents online.

Example 1

According to the passage, what is the earliest that people start their Christmas shopping?

A   In the preceding summer
B   In the preceding October
C   In the preceding November
D   Christmas Eve
E   In early December

The correct answer is A. This has already been marked in Example 1 in the Comprehension section of your answer sheet.

Practice Question 1

In recent years, what has caused a change in how people shop?

A   There are more shops
B   Shops are more crowded
C   You can easily organise your journey to the shops
D   New products are available
E   There has been a rise in use of the Internet

The correct answer is E. Please mark this in Practice Question 1 in the Comprehension section of your answer sheet.

STOP AND WAIT FOR FURTHER INSTRUCTIONS

Read the following passage, then answer the questions below.

The Georgian House

While sitting in their lounge, Helen and John both realised that their once beautifully decorated home had become uninspiring, tired and unfashionable.

"Are you thinking what I am thinking John?" Helen asked tentatively. "Yes, the lounge looks shabby and I am not sure that it looks special anymore," said John. The lounge had been designed with exquisite taste, and represented the pinnacle of Helen's talents, but it was now a shadow of its former self.

Helen had always been artistically minded and had initially wanted to be an interior designer. However, she had never managed to realise her dream. She loved colour and texture, and often changed the interior of her home according to the passing whims of fashion. She enjoyed redecorating her lounge walls in a more fashionable colour scheme. She was generally inspired by different, and often unusual influences. Sometimes, it would be the colour of an outfit which her friend was wearing, or the colour scheme featured in a magazine advertisement. On occasions, Helen had stayed in five-star hotels, which had so inspired her that she wanted to replicate the ambience in her home. However, she had recently been too busy to notice, as her elderly uncle had been suffering with a chronic illness, and she had been busy tending to his needs. The room which she had previously been so proud of, had now deteriorated.

Helen set to work to rejuvenate her lounge. The room continued to be important as her family spent most of their recreational time there. She decided that she would remove the existing colour scheme of red and gold, and would replace it with soft blue and grey hues that had become fashionable in recent years. The problem that she now faced was the carpet, which was coral in colour, and the rug which was gold and brown.

The next morning she rolled up the rug and placed it outside her front door with a note saying, "Please take!"

She then single-handedly pulled up the carpet. Instantly, the lounge appeared fresher. She realised that the room now looked much larger, and that the coral carpet had been quite oppressive.

Helen was now unsure as to how she should tackle what had become a rather large project. She thought how lucky it was that she did not have to remove any wallpaper.

Helen then bought some small samples of paint at her local ironmongers. The shopkeeper had seen the extensive collection of paint samples and had given her some good advice.

"Here is a little secret that only the best designers know." Helen was sure that she would know his secret. However, she was surprised when she learnt something new. "When deciding on the shade of paint, the only way you really and truly get an idea of how it is going to look, is by painting sample areas in the corners of the room".

CONTINUE WORKING

Helen was amazed that she had never thought of this! As she wandered home, happily swinging her hessian bag, she listened to the clattering of the paint pots. She relished the thought of removing the faded grandeur of her lounge and replacing it with exquisite colours which would highlight the traditional features of her rather wonderful Georgian house.

1 What does 'a shadow of its former self' mean?

    A   More selfless
    B   Less impressive
    C   More showing
    D   Less tasteful
    E   Less oppressive

2 What is Helen's job?

    A   Interior designer
    B   Fashion designer
    C   Advertising executive
    D   Doctor
    E   Passage does not say

3 Which of these phrases is mentioned as having inspired Helen in the past?

    A   A hospital in which her uncle had been recovering
    B   Advertisements on the television
    C   Restaurants which she had visited
    D   Colourful clothes and luxurious hotels
    E   Photographs in shop windows

4 What did Helen do with the carpet?

    A   She wrote a note and attached it to the carpet
    B   She rolled it up and put it outside
    C   She removed it on her own
    D   It was left 'in situ'
    E   It was replaced with a new carpet

5 What is the meaning of the word 'chronic'?

    A   Occurring in later life
    B   Occurring on the weekend
    C   Occurring at intermittent intervals
    D   Occurring for a short period
    E   Occurring for a long period

CONTINUE WORKING

(6) What type of word is 'pinnacle'?

A   Verb
B   Noun
C   Adjective
D   Adverb
E   Pronoun

(7) Why had Helen not noticed that her lounge had become shabby?

A   Due to her many recreational activities
B   Due to being on holiday
C   Due to designing advertisements
D   Due to staying in five-star hotels
E   Due to a family member being ill

(8) Why was Helen's lounge so important?

A   Due to the wallpaper
B   Due to her elderly uncle coming to stay
C   Due to the proximity to the kitchen
D   Due to it being the place where her family spent their time
E   Due to Helen's deterioration

(9) What did Helen learn from the shopkeeper?

A   A tradition
B   A design secret
C   Some upsetting news
D   A new piece of fabric
E   A new carpet

(10) What colours did Helen want to use in her rejuvenated lounge?

A   Grey and red tones
B   Coral and grey tones
C   Blue and coral tones
D   Red and gold tones
E   Grey and blue tones

STOP AND WAIT FOR FURTHER INSTRUCTIONS

Shuffled Sentences

INSTRUCTIONS

YOU HAVE 10 MINUTES TO COMPLETE THE FOLLOWING SECTION.

YOU HAVE 15 QUESTIONS TO COMPLETE WITHIN THE TIME GIVEN.

EXAMPLES

Example 1

The following sentence is shuffled and also contains one unnecessary word.
Rearrange the sentence correctly, in order to identify the unnecessary word.

dog the ran fetch the to stick gluing.

A	B	C	D	E
gluing	dog	ran	the	stick

The correct answer is A. This has already been marked in Example 1 in the Shuffled Sentences section of your answer sheet.

Practice Question 1

The following sentence is shuffled and also contains one unnecessary word.
Rearrange the sentence correctly, in order to identify the unnecessary word.

pushed Emma stood up and closed the table under the chair.

A	B	C	D	E
chair	stood	under	closed	Emma

The correct answer is D. Please mark this in Practice Question 1 in the Shuffled Sentences section of your answer sheet.

STOP AND WAIT FOR FURTHER INSTRUCTIONS

Each sentence below is shuffled and also contains one unnecessary word.
Rearrange each sentence correctly, in order to identify the unnecessary word.

1 he sitting in his bought morning that the engine enjoyed boy car which had.

A	B	C	D	E
the	in	engine	car	boy

2 biscuit despite awful hungry was still girl eating her the last.

A	B	C	D	E
biscuit	the	her	awful	last

3 like which brand music we listening to show radio classical the plays.

A	B	C	D	E
show	brand	listening	which	plays

4 a dancer young became talented the a man training result as extend of his.

A	B	C	D	E
dancer	became	of	result	extend

5 gardening courageous most according people to is exercise good.

A	B	C	D	E
courageous	to	is	gardening	exercise

6 promptly overhead the started competition despite o' clock ten at quietly thunderstorm the.

A	B	C	D	E
the	at	quietly	overhead	despite

7 house lengthy reading completed he finally novel the.

A	B	C	D	E
he	and	completed	novel	house

CONTINUE WORKING

8 ways according many you in scientists for eggs good are some to severe.

A	B	C	D	E
some	severe	good	for	ways

9 day dentists teeth flossed recommend brushing a twice your all.

A	B	C	D	E
all	a	day	flossed	twice

10 electric and singers chargeable was atmosphere the the amazing were.

A	B	C	D	E
chargeable	singers	and	the	electric

11 milk I out still although heavily have supermarket the I been run today to have of.

A	B	C	D	E
I	today	heavily	out	still

12 attractive arranged designer the sketch interior an has produced.

A	B	C	D	E
arranged	designer	of	the	house

13 forward wonderful standard we looking had time we our to not were party aunt's a but.

A	B	C	D	E
looking	a	to	our	standard

14 barking awoken most neighbours threw the the by of were dog.

A	B	C	D	E
barking	by	the	threw	most

15 calm needs overgrown the mowing grass garden the in.

A	B	C	D	E
calm	needs	for	garden	in

STOP AND WAIT FOR FURTHER INSTRUCTIONS ⊗

Numeracy

INSTRUCTIONS

 YOU HAVE 6 MINUTES TO COMPLETE THE FOLLOWING SECTION.

YOU HAVE 13 QUESTIONS TO COMPLETE WITHIN THE TIME GIVEN.

EXAMPLES

The questions within this section are not multiple choice. Write the answer to each question on the answer sheet by selecting the correct digits from the columns provided.

Example 1

Calculate 14 + 23

The correct answer is 37. This has already been marked in Example 1 in the Numeracy section of your answer sheet.

Practice Question 1

Calculate 83 – 75

The correct answer is 8. Please mark this in Practice Question 1 in the Numeracy section of your answer sheet. Note that a single-digit answer should be marked with a 0 in the left-hand column, so mark 08 on your answer sheet.

STOP AND WAIT FOR FURTHER INSTRUCTIONS

(1) How many days are there between the following 2 dates (inclusive):

3rd February 2015 to 2nd March 2015

(2) How many weeks in 56 days?

(3) Look at the picture of the triangle.

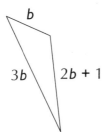

If $b = 3$, calculate the length of the perimeter in centimetres.

(4) I walk at 2.5 mph. The bus stop is 0.5 miles away from home. How long in minutes is the walk from home to the bus stop?

(5) Two years ago Jenny was two years younger than Kate. If Kate is now 12, how old is Jenny?

(6) Select the appropriate number or numbers to complete the sequence in place of the ? in the brackets below.

(36, 20, 12, 8, ?, 5)

(7) What is the 18th term in the following series:

105, 100, 95, 90, 85...

(8) The petrol tank in my car is currently $\frac{2}{3}$ full. The capacity of the tank is 84 litres. How many more litres will it hold?

(9) Calculate the number of 200 ml cups I can fill from a 1.5 litre bottle of water.

(10) How many quarters of an hour are there in 180 minutes?

(11) How many vertices are there on a triangular prism?

(12) Calculate the following:

$8 + (2 \times 13)$

(13) Calculate the following:

$583 - 495$

STOP AND WAIT FOR FURTHER INSTRUCTIONS ⊗

Problem Solving

 INSTRUCTIONS

 YOU HAVE 10 MINUTES TO COMPLETE THE FOLLOWING SECTION.

YOU HAVE 10 QUESTIONS TO COMPLETE WITHIN THE TIME GIVEN.

EXAMPLES

A £2.60	B £3.40	C £2.40	D 25	E £1.35
F £3.40	G 14	H 31	I 28	J 34

Example 1

Calculate the following:

If I buy five apples at 20p each, and four bananas at 35p each, how much change will I receive if I pay with a £5 note.

The correct answer is A. This has already been marked in Example 1 in the Problem Solving section of your answer sheet.

Practice Question 1

Calculate the following:

There are 17 people on a bus when it arrives at a bus stop. Eleven people get on the bus, and three get off. How many people are then left on the bus?

The correct answer is D. Please mark this in Practice Question 1 in the Problem Solving section of your answer sheet.

STOP AND WAIT FOR FURTHER INSTRUCTIONS

A £450	B 3	C 24	D £28,900	E £25,000
F £1,200	G 12	H £1,100	I £150	J 13

Select an answer to each question from the 10 different possible answers in the table above.
You may use an answer for more than one question.

(1) Alison is having a new kitchen put into her house. The kitchen is supposed to be fitted by 4 men who will complete the kitchen in 6 days. However, only 2 of the men are available to fit the kitchen. If all of the men work at the same speed, how many days will it take the 2 men to fit the kitchen?

(2) The floor is slightly larger than before as the kitchen has been extended. The floor now measures 6 m in length by 4 m in width. How many metres squared is the area of the floor now?

(3) The floor is to be covered with large square tiles. Each edge of a tile measures 50 cm. How many boxes of tiles are required, if each box contains 40 tiles?

(4) The new oven has a discount of 25% as it is in the sale. The original price was £600. What is the discount on the oven?

(5) Alison borrowed £20,000 from the bank to pay for the new kitchen extension. The bank charges Alison interest of 6% each year on the amount that she borrowed. How much interest does the bank charge each year?

(6) The fridge has $\frac{1}{3}$ off the original price, as it too is in the sale. If the sale price is £300, what was the original price?

(7) The planning and building of the kitchen extension took three months in total. How many weeks was this?

(8) When completed, the new extended kitchen cost £21,100 in total. How much more was this than the amount Alison first borrowed from the bank?

(9) Alison is planning to sell her house. Before the kitchen extension, she had her house valued. It was valued then at £200,000. The house was valued again after the extension at £250,000. Taking into account how much Alison spent on her new kitchen, how much will Alison gain from the new kitchen extension, if she sells the house for the new value?

(10) The new value of Alison's house after the extension is 10 times the price paid when she bought the house 34 years ago. How much did Alison pay for the house 34 years ago?

STOP AND WAIT FOR FURTHER INSTRUCTIONS

Synonyms

INSTRUCTIONS

 YOU HAVE 5 MINUTES TO COMPLETE THE FOLLOWING SECTION.

YOU HAVE 23 QUESTIONS TO COMPLETE WITHIN THE TIME GIVEN.

EXAMPLES

Example 1

Select the word that is most similar in meaning to the following word:

cold

A	B	C	D	E
collect	fence	foggy	windy	chilly

The correct answer is E. This has already been marked in Example 1 in the Synonyms section of your answer sheet.

Practice Question 1

Select the word that is most similar in meaning to the following word:

start

A	B	C	D	E
cramped	begin	free	without	change

The correct answer is B. Please mark this in Practice Question 1 in the Synonyms section of your answer sheet.

STOP AND WAIT FOR FURTHER INSTRUCTIONS

Select the word from each table that is most similar in meaning to the word above the table.

1 pitiful

A	B	C	D	E
deep	fanciful	insignificant	gleeful	serene

2 curvature

A	B	C	D	E
straight	arc	duplicate	certain	treasured

3 misfortune

A	B	C	D	E
tiresome	carefully	transfer	setback	boast

4 futile

A	B	C	D	E
lush	assess	determined	timid	ineffective

5 escarpment

A	B	C	D	E
cliff	absurd	dip	average	mandatory

6 woe

A	B	C	D	E
courage	triumph	boredom	civility	anguish

7 perpendicular

A	B	C	D	E
familiar	violet	upright	aspect	decline

CONTINUE WORKING

8 outside

A	B	C	D	E
unravel	ending	exterior	core	revolve

9 slight

A	B	C	D	E
traitor	grand	scent	observe	slender

10 void

A	B	C	D	E
prevent	gap	foil	lavish	equilibrium

11 peculiar

A	B	C	D	E
loyal	spectacular	curious	frantic	eruption

12 talented

A	B	C	D	E
passage	ordinary	distorted	accomplished	incompetent

13 union

A	B	C	D	E
alliance	resolve	ambition	distraction	repetition

14 particulars

A	B	C	D	E
role	resumption	details	senses	revolutions

15 quirky

A	B	C	D	E
menace	unconventional	liable	agility	smirk

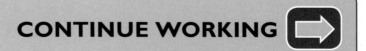

CONTINUE WORKING

16 sour

A	B	C	D	E
charming	ponder	acrimonious	trusted	delightful

17 compound

A	B	C	D	E
blend	conquer	rise	beaming	inscription

18 utmost

A	B	C	D	E
utter	lest	exterior	moisten	ultimate

19 flourish

A	B	C	D	E
thrive	wither	fragment	imitate	flawed

20 neutral

A	B	C	D	E
indifferent	navigation	drab	deduct	sift

21 type

A	B	C	D	E
embed	ability	attire	contact	mode

22 spectacle

A	B	C	D	E
spiritual	pound	parade	improvise	analysis

23 estimate

A	B	C	D	E
projection	quarrel	engagement	supple	deterioration

STOP AND WAIT FOR FURTHER INSTRUCTIONS

Non-Verbal Reasoning

 YOU HAVE 6 MINUTES TO COMPLETE THE FOLLOWING SECTION.

YOU HAVE 14 QUESTIONS TO COMPLETE WITHIN THE TIME GIVEN.

EXAMPLES

COMPLETE THE SEQUENCE Example 1

Select the picture from the bottom row that will complete the sequence in place of the ? in the top row.

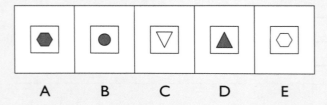

The correct answer is C. This has already been marked in Example 1 in the Non-Verbal Reasoning section of your answer sheet.

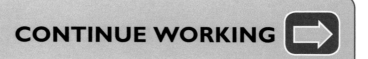 **CONTINUE WORKING**

COMPLETE THE SEQUENCE Practice Question 1

Select the picture from the bottom row that will complete the sequence in place of the ? in the top row.

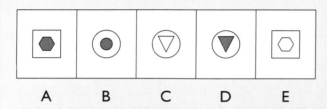

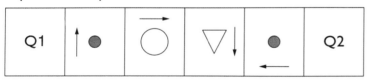

A   B   C   D   E

The correct answer is D. Please mark this in Practice Question 1 in the Non-Verbal Reasoning section of your answer sheet.

STOP AND WAIT FOR FURTHER INSTRUCTIONS ⊗

Select the correct pictures from the bottom row in order to finish the incomplete sequence on the top row. One picture should be chosen for Q1 and another picture for Q2.

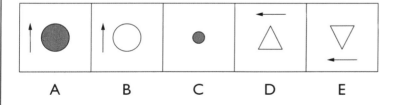

A   B   C   D   E

CONTINUE WORKING ⇨

Select the correct pictures from the bottom row in order to finish the incomplete sequence on the top row. One picture should be chosen for Q3 and another picture for Q4.

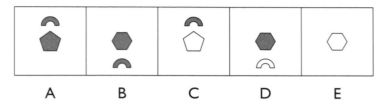

Select the correct pictures from the bottom row in order to finish the incomplete sequence on the top row. One picture should be chosen for Q5 and another picture for Q6.

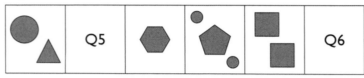

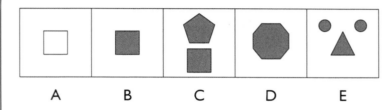

Select the correct pictures from the bottom row in order to finish the incomplete sequence on the top row. One picture should be chosen for Q7 and another picture for Q8.

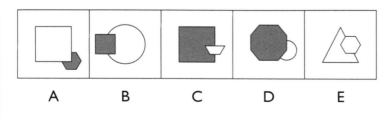

CONTINUE WORKING ⇨

Select the correct pictures from the bottom row in order to finish the incomplete sequence on the top row. One picture should be chosen for Q9 and another picture for Q10.

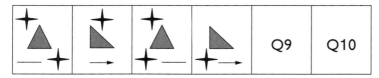

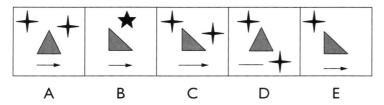

A B C D E

Select the correct pictures from the bottom row in order to finish the incomplete sequence on the top row. One picture should be chosen for Q11 and another picture for Q12.

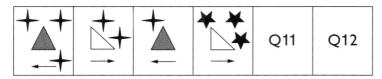

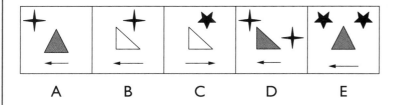

A B C D E

Select the correct pictures from the bottom row in order to finish the incomplete sequence on the top row. One picture should be chosen for Q13 and another picture for Q14.

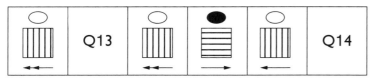

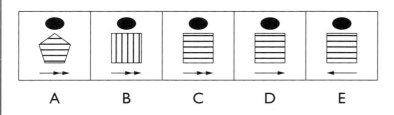

A B C D E

END OF PAPER

Test B Paper 2

Instructions

1. Ensure you have pencils and an eraser with you.

2. Make sure you are able to see a clock or watch.

3. Write your name on the answer sheet.

4. Do not open the question booklet until you are told to do so by the audio instructions.

5. Listen carefully to the audio instructions given.

6. Mark your answers on the answer sheet only.

7. All workings must be completed on a separate piece of paper.

8. You should not use a calculator, dictionary or thesaurus at any point in this paper.

9. Move through the paper as quickly as possible and with care.

10. Follow the instructions at the foot of each page.

11. You should mark your answers with a horizontal strike, as shown on the answer sheet.

12. If you want to change your answer, ensure that you rub out your first answer and that your second answer is clearly more visible.

13. You can go back and review any questions that are within the section you are working on only. You must await further instructions before moving onto another section.

Symbols and Phrases used in the Tests

 Instructions  Time allowed for this section Stop and wait for further instructions Continue working

Problem Solving

 YOU HAVE 12 MINUTES TO COMPLETE THE FOLLOWING SECTION.

YOU HAVE 10 QUESTIONS TO COMPLETE WITHIN THE TIME GIVEN.

EXAMPLES

A	B	C	D	E	F	G	H	I	J
£2.60	£3.40	£2.40	25	£1.35	£3.40	14	31	28	34

Example 1

Calculate the following:

If I buy 5 apples at 20p each and 4 bananas at 35p each, how much change will I receive if I pay with a £5 note?

The correct answer is A. This has been marked in Example 1 in the Problem Solving section of your answer sheet.

Practice Question 1

Calculate the following:

There are 17 people on a bus when it arrives at a bus stop.
11 people get on the bus and 3 get off. How many people are then left on the bus?

The correct answer is D. Please mark the answer D in the Problem Solving section of your answer sheet.

STOP AND WAIT FOR FURTHER INSTRUCTIONS

Several questions will follow for you to answer.

A	B	C	D	E	F	G	H	I	J
£500	06:00	8	17:00	9	05:00	£20	£1,100	£550	10

Select an answer to each question from the possible answers in the table above.
You may use an answer for more than one question.

① Sara and her family are going on a two-week holiday to Australia. Sara is married to Jack. They have two children, Greg and Horace, aged 15 and 13 respectively at the time of the holiday. The flights to Australia from their home in London cost £3,300 in total for the family of four. If the adult tickets were twice the price of the child tickets, how much did the flights for each child cost? (Child tickets are for under-16s.)

② The flight stops in Singapore before refuelling to continue to Sydney, Australia. The stopover time in Singapore is three hours before taking off again for Sydney. Take off is scheduled for 09:00 on 21 December 2015 from London. The flight is due to arrive in Singapore at 07:00 (Singapore time) the following day. Singapore is eight hours ahead of London. If the flight time to Sydney from Singapore is five hours, when is the flight scheduled to arrive in Sydney using Sydney time, which is two hours ahead of Singapore?

③ How many hours ahead of London is Sydney?

④ Passengers in London were able to check-in at the airport three hours before the scheduled take-off time. What time could passengers on the London to Sydney flight check-in from?

⑤ The family organised a taxi to collect them from their London home in Putney, one hour before the earliest check-in time. The taxi collected the family on time. What time was this?

⑥ The exchange rate at the time the family purchased some travellers cheques in Australian Dollars, was $1.75 (Australian Dollars):£1 (British Pounds).

Excluding any transaction fee, how much did it cost the family in pounds to buy $1,925 (Australian Dollars)?

⑦ The family also changed some British pounds into Australian Dollars before they left London at the same rate ($1.75:£1). They received $875 in Australian Dollars. Excluding any transaction fee, how much did this cost them in pounds?

CONTINUE WORKING

(8) Horace bought some surf shorts in Sydney out of the money changed before they left London. The shorts were originally $70. They were on sale with a discount on the original price of 50%. How much did the surf shorts cost Horace in British Pounds?

(9) On the flight from London bound for Sydney, there were 468 passengers who boarded the flight in London. Fifteen of these passengers only had tickets to Singapore, as this was their final destination. If 461 passengers arrived in Sydney, how many passengers boarded the plane for the first leg of their journey in Singapore?

(10) Whilst queuing for the Sydney Aquarium, Greg saw one of his old school friends, Ian Baldwin, who he had not seen since Christmas in 2005. Approximately how many years is it since Greg last saw Ian Baldwin?

STOP AND WAIT FOR FURTHER INSTRUCTIONS

Cloze

INSTRUCTIONS

 YOU HAVE 10 MINUTES TO COMPLETE THE FOLLOWING SECTION.

YOU HAVE 20 QUESTIONS TO COMPLETE WITHIN THE TIME GIVEN.

EXAMPLES

Example 1

Read the sentence below and select the most appropriate word from the table.

A	B	C	D	E
backdrop	carefully	drawer	disadvantage	dilution

The undulating hills were the perfect Q1 _____ for the watercolour painting.

Please select your answer to go in the place of Q1 in the sentence above.

The correct answer is A. This has already been marked in Example 1 in the Cloze section of your answer sheet.

Practice Question 1

Read the sentence below and select the most appropriate word from the table.

A	B	C	D	E
had	interior	success	attend	absent

The girl decided she would like to Q2 _____ the party.

Please select your answer to go in the place of Q2 in the sentence above.

The correct answer is D. Please mark the answer D in Practice Question 1 in the Cloze section of your answer sheet.

STOP AND WAIT FOR FURTHER INSTRUCTIONS

Read the following passage and select the most appropriate word from the table below by choosing the letter above the word. There are 10 questions. For example, Q1 is where you should put your answer to Question 1 on your answer sheet.

A	B	C	D	E
forming	unearthed	technical	visiting	carefully
F	**G**	**H**	**I**	**J**
apparent	advertisement	graveyard	guided	remote

An Archaeologist's Response

Dear Mrs Bates,

I would like to confirm my interest in your Q1 _____ for an archaeologist working on the site in Northamptonshire.

As stated in the job description, I would be happy to work on a contract basis with the hope of eventually Q2 _____ part of your core team of archaeologists.

I have previous experience on archaeological digs around the UK and also overseas. I am skilled in the necessary Q3 _____ knowledge required when on site.

I worked for a number of weeks on a project where Roman remains were found in a Q4 _____ field in Worcestershire. Once we had started the dig, it became Q5 _____ that the site was of great interest and importance. In the last few weeks of the dig, we Q6 _____ a previously undiscovered mosaic. The tesserae were Q7 _____ removed and were then placed in a local museum.

I then worked on a project in a Q8 _____ in London. I was a member of a team who were part of a 'rescue archaeology' project. We had no longer than four weeks to excavate and record the findings within the graveyard, before the developers built a teashop on the site. I learned a great deal from this project and was pleased to have been chosen to work on such a prestigious project of national importance.

I would also like to state that at various points in time, I have been asked to provide Q9 _____ tours for amateur archaeologists Q10 _____ the sites. I would be very happy to provide this service, should you wish me to assist in this way.

Yours sincerely,

Max Granger

CONTINUE WORKING

Read the following passage and select the most appropriate word from the table below, by selecting the letter above the word. There are 10 questions. For example, Q11 is where you should put your answer to Question 11 on your answer sheet.

A	B	C	D	E
provisions	treacherous	necessary	working	reputable
F	**G**	**H**	**I**	**J**
tow	breakdown	estimated	travelling	motorists

Instructions for the Winter Months

Q11 _____ by car in the winter months is a concern for many
Q12 _____ and can add to the statistics for weather-related deaths. Here are some guidelines for consideration when driving in sub-zero conditions.

- What should you take with you on a long journey?

  You should take a shovel in case you are stuck in a snowdrift.

  Take blankets and enough clothing layers to keep you warm in the event of a
  Q13 _____ .

  Take some food and drinks with you. It is not uncommon for traffic to be at a standstill for many hours and so you should have Q14 _____ with you for that occurrence.

- What happens if you breakdown?

  Do you have cover from a Q15 _____ company which you can contact in the event of a breakdown? Would you want them to Q16 _____ your car to the nearest garage or would you want them to take you to your home? How much will this cost?

- Is there anything else you can do to prepare for your journey?

  If you know that the conditions are Q17 _____ then snow chains for your wheels are recommended.

  Contact the person who you are travelling to see, and tell them your
  Q18 _____ time of arrival.

- Is your car in good Q19 _____ order?

  Check your oil levels and make sure you have more than enough fuel to reach your destination.

  Avoid travelling unless it is absolutely Q20 _____ .

STOP AND WAIT FOR FURTHER INSTRUCTIONS

Non-Verbal Reasoning

INSTRUCTIONS

 YOU HAVE 8 MINUTES TO COMPLETE THE FOLLOWING SECTION.

YOU HAVE 13 QUESTIONS TO COMPLETE WITHIN THE TIME GIVEN.

EXAMPLES

CUBE NET Example 1

Look at the cube net. Select the only cube that could be formed from the net below.

The correct answer is E. This has already been marked in Example 1 in the Non-Verbal Reasoning section of your answer sheet.

A B C D E

CUBE NET Practice Question 1

Look at the cube net. Select the only cube that could be formed from the net below.

The correct answer is A. Please mark this in Practice Question 1 in the Non-Verbal Reasoning section of your answer sheet.

A B C D E

CONTINUE WORKING

LEAST SIMILAR Example 2

Select the image that is least similar to the other images.

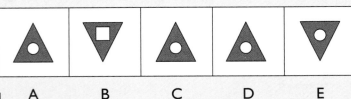

A   B   C   D   E

The correct answer is B. This has already been marked in Example 2 in the Non-Verbal Reasoning section of your answer sheet.

LEAST SIMILAR Practice Question 2

Select the image that is least similar to the other images.

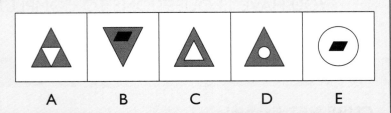

A   B   C   D   E

The correct answer is E. Please mark this in Practice Question 2 in the Non-Verbal Reasoning section of your answer sheet.

STOP AND WAIT FOR FURTHER INSTRUCTIONS

(1) Select the image that is least similar to the other images.

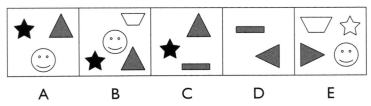

A   B   C   D   E

(2) Select the image that is least similar to the other images.

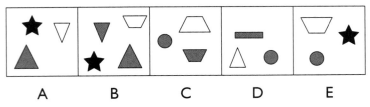

A   B   C   D   E

CONTINUE WORKING

3 Select the image that is least similar to the other images.

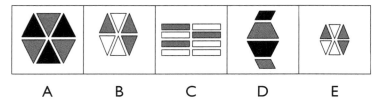

    A   B   C   D   E

4 Select the image that is least similar to the other images.

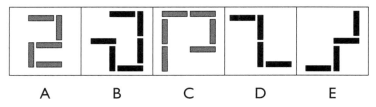

    A   B   C   D   E

5 Select the image that is least similar to the other images.

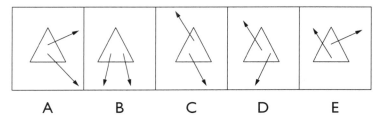

    A   B   C   D   E

6 Select the image that is least similar to the other images.

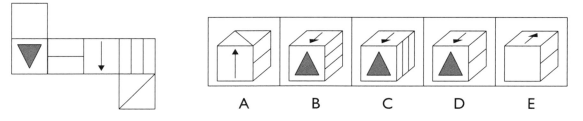

    A   B   C   D   E

7 Look at the cube net. Select the only cube that could be formed from the net.

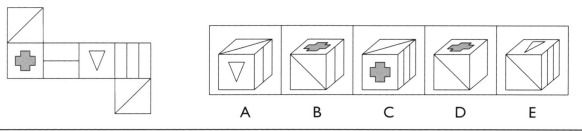

    A   B   C   D   E

8 Look at the cube net. Select the only cube that could be formed from the net.

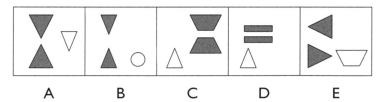

    A   B   C   D   E

CONTINUE WORKING ⏩

9 Look at the cube net. Select the only cube that could be formed from the net.

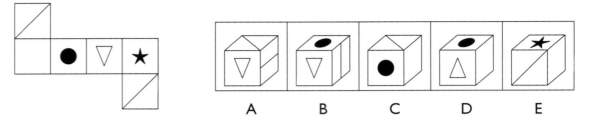

10 Look at the cube net. Select the only cube that could be formed from the net.

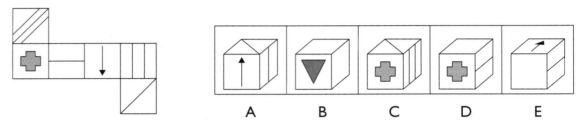

11 Look at the cube net. Select the only cube that could be formed from the net.

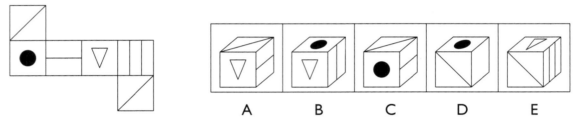

12 Look at the cube net. Select the only cube that could be formed from the net.

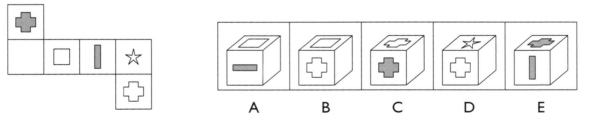

13 Look at the cube net. Select the only cube that could be formed from the net.

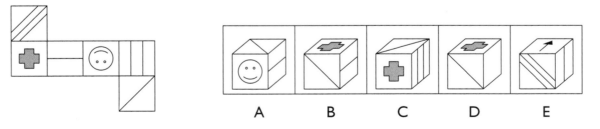

STOP AND WAIT FOR FURTHER INSTRUCTIONS

Antonyms

 INSTRUCTIONS

 YOU HAVE 5 MINUTES TO COMPLETE THE FOLLOWING SECTION.

YOU HAVE 15 QUESTIONS TO COMPLETE WITHIN THE TIME GIVEN.

EXAMPLES

Example 1

Select the word that is least similar to the following word:

light

A	B	C	D	E
dark	water	feather	bright	hill

The correct answer is A dark. This has already been marked in Example 1 in the Antonyms section of your answer sheet.

Practice Question 1

Select the word that is least similar to the following word:

smooth

A	B	C	D	E
allow	beneath	rough	whilst	shade

The correct answer is C rough. Please mark the answer C in Practice Question 1 in the Antonyms section of your answer sheet.

STOP AND WAIT FOR FURTHER INSTRUCTIONS

In each row, select the word from the table that is least similar to the word above the table.

(1) interested

A	B	C	D	E
straight	animated	apathetic	vivid	decent

(2) lush

A	B	C	D	E
barren	just	reliable	frank	jovial

(3) durable

A	B	C	D	E
irritable	unreliable	upbeat	agitated	bustling

(4) detect

A	B	C	D	E
delicate	slight	find	flaw	hide

(5) eschew

A	B	C	D	E
shun	dodge	embrace	avoid	order

(6) agreement

A	B	C	D	E
harmony	dispute	unison	chorus	compatible

CONTINUE WORKING ⏵

7 accumulate

A	B	C	D	E
hoard	divide	regime	readiness	vague

8 arid

A	B	C	D	E
serene	barren	fertile	review	design

9 replica

A	B	C	D	E
regain	original	defence	greet	inhabitant

10 solo

A	B	C	D	E
isolation	typhoon	titan	refuge	combined

11 sorrow

A	B	C	D	E
obnoxious	cheer	externally	dissect	grief

12 dirty

A	B	C	D	E
intensive	apparent	purify	vivid	gaudy

CONTINUE WORKING ⇨

(13) delicious

A	B	C	D	E
precedence	quibble	variable	appetising	bland

(14) naïve

A	B	C	D	E
revive	experienced	tactful	uphold	headway

(15) demote

A	B	C	D	E
distinctly	upgrade	impulse	elevate	contort

STOP AND WAIT FOR FURTHER INSTRUCTIONS ✖

Numeracy

 INSTRUCTIONS

 YOU HAVE 10 MINUTES TO COMPLETE THE FOLLOWING SECTION.

YOU HAVE 18 QUESTIONS TO COMPLETE WITHIN THE TIME GIVEN.

EXAMPLES

The questions within this section are not multiple-choice. Write the answer to each question on the answer sheet by selecting the correct digits from the columns provided.

Example 1

Calculate 14 + 23

The correct answer is 37. This has already been marked in Example 1 in the Numeracy section of your answer sheet.

Practice Question 1

Calculate 83 – 75

The correct answer is 8. Write the answer in Practice Question 1 in the Numeracy section of the answer sheet. Note that a single-digit answer should be marked with a 0 in the left-hand column, so mark 08 on your answer sheet.

STOP AND WAIT FOR FURTHER INSTRUCTIONS

(1) Calculate the following:

274 − 175

(2) Find the missing number to replace ? to make the equation correct:

47 − 14 = 3 × ?

(3) Calculate the next number in the following sequence:

7, 8, 10, 13, 17, ?

(4) What is the number if 61 is 3 less than 8 times the number?

(5) Look at the Venn Diagram showing information about children in a class.

Children

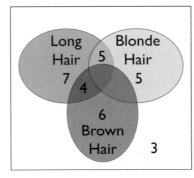

How many of the children had long hair, blonde hair or brown hair?

(6) How many days are in September?

(7) Calculate the following:

−12 + 19

(8) What is the range of the following shoe sizes:

3, 5, 7, 2, 8, 6, 3, 4, 5, 7, 4, 1, 6, 9, 4

CONTINUE WORKING

(9) Jackie paid £64 for a bike after a 20% discount. What was the original price in £ of the bike?

(10) Find the value of y if:

$21 - y = 2y$

(11) Jay has three times as many cards as Judy. Judy has twice as many as Martin. There are 252 cards in total. How many cards does Judy have?

(12) Calculate:

91 divided by 7

(13) How many sixths of a cake are there in three whole cakes?

(14) What is the smallest number of coins from which I could make £2.89 exactly?

(15) If eight children have each received seven Christmas cards, how many Christmas cards have the eight children received in total?

(16) If the temperature on 2 January was −3°C, and the temperature on 7 January was −11°C, by how many °C had the temperature dropped between these two dates?

(17) There are twice as many teachers in Woodchurch Primary School as there were 20 years ago. There are 14 teachers currently. How many teachers were there 20 years ago?

(18) In five years' time, I will be nine years younger than my older sister and my older sister will be a third of my mother's age. My mother is 40 now. How old am I now?

END OF PAPER

Answers to Test A Paper 1

Comprehension

Q1 *C*
The caves are just under 18,000 years old, so the correct option is less than 20,000 years old

Q2 *E*
The vast majority of the paintings are of animals

Q3 *A*
To allow the caves to be preserved

Q4 *D*
Fragments of sculptures and large buildings

Q5 *A*
In Italy

Q6 *B*
Paintings looked more realistic

Q7 *E*
To make an investment

Q8 *B*
Art placed in an area to benefit a community, or newly developed area

Q9 *E*
Noticeable

Q10 *D*
Modern art is often controversial

Shuffled Sentences

Q1 *C*
reserve
I think the book is better than the film.

Q2 *A*
paint
She drew the curtains to keep the warmth in.

Q3 *A*
play
The record number of claims kept the insurance firm busy.

Q4 *C*
up
The duck down pillows are more comfortable.

Q5 *D*
dough
You need to be quick to answer the question.

Q6 *E since*
Despite the weather the barbecue went ahead.

Q7 *D*
horse
The building was not stable following the earthquake.

Q8 *A*
stair
The girl continued to stare up at her.

Q9 *C*
blind
She drew a deep breath before beginning her speech.

Q10 *B*
tried
The sofa was looking tired after a number of years of use.

Q11 *E*
rain
The reign of the current monarch was coming to an end.

Q12 *B*
small
Roger kicked the ball through the window.

Q13 *C*
in
The accident caused heavy traffic on the motorway.

Q14 *A*
earlier
Jon is due to meet Eva at noon.

Q15 *D*
light
The guests felt rather bloated after their substantial dinner.

Numeracy

Q1 *(11)*
3 × 5 = 15, 15 − 4 = 11 uses order of operations rules BODMAS

Q2 *(22)*
4 ÷ 2 = 2, 24 − 2 = 22 uses order of operations rules BODMAS

Q3 *(16)*
6 ÷ 3 = 2, 18 − 2 = 16 uses order of operations rules BODMAS

Q4 *(03)*
1 + 2 = 3 The next number is the sum of the last 2 numbers (Fibonacci sequence).

Q5 *(13)*
range is highest value less the lowest value, 14 − 1 = 13

Q6 *(17)*
When 17 is divided by 7 there is a remainder of 3.

Q7 *(19)*
This does not divide exactly into 63, as there is a remainder of 6.

Q8 *(06)*
This is the only factor of both 18 and 48.

Q9 *(03)*
n + 3 = n + n (n is my age now) so n = 3

Q10 *(12)*
Alan is 11 now, so will be 12 in 1 year from now.

Q11 *(07)*
April is month 4, November is month 11, so 11 − 4 = 7 months.

Q12 *(39)*
There are exactly 52 weeks in a non-leap year, which is 12 months long.
So in 3 months, or quarter of a year, there will be 52 ÷ 4 = 13 weeks, and in 9 months there are 52 − 13 = 39 weeks.

Q13 *(43)*
We are looking for a number which is 7 more than a multiple of 9, and between 40 and 50. Try these multiples of 9 : 27, 36, 45. When 7 is added to each, this gives: 34, 43 and 52, so 43 is the only answer between 40 and 50.

Problem Solving

Q1 *D*
2 : 3 : 5
Simplifying the ratio 10 : 15 : 25 (by dividing by 5)

Q2 *B*
6 minutes.
I actually finish buying coffee at 7.40 am. The only answer option that means the train departs at or after 7.40 is B.

Q3 *E*
12
60% girls, so 40% must be boys; 10% of 30 is 3, so 40% of 30 is 4 × 3 = 12

Q4 *A*
21
60% of (30 + 5). 10% of 35 is 3.5, 60% of 35 is 6 × 3.5 = 21

Q5 *D*
2 : 3
40% boys 60% girls, 14 boys and 21 girls, simplifies to 2 : 3 (by dividing by 7)

Q6 *A*
Just under 20 minutes
3 buses every hour or 60 minutes, means one bus every 20 minutes as they are always on time. If you just missed a bus, you would have just under 20 minutes to wait until the next bus.

Q7 *C*
10 minutes
The longest is 20 minutes and shortest is 0 minutes, so the average time is $\frac{(0 + 20)}{2} = 10$ minutes.

Q8 *D*
9 mph
3 miles in 20 minutes means the bus travels 9 miles in 60 minutes, so 9 miles per hour.

Q9 *A*
6 hrs 35 mins, 2 hours 50 plus 3 hours 45 mins, from 9:10 a.m. to 3:45 p.m.

Q10 *E*
girls 1329, boys 1320, teachers 198, Boys = 2847 (all) − 1527(teachers and girls) = 1320

Synonyms

Q1 *E* plenty		**Q13** *B* dependent
Q2 *B* calm		**Q14** *D* convex
Q3 *C* inflexible		**Q15** *A* apathetic
Q4 *D* volatile		**Q16** *D* crate
Q5 *E* sad		**Q17** *D* gnarled
Q6 *A* spiral		**Q18** *C* injure
Q7 *B* unintelligent		**Q19** *C* optimistic
Q8 *C* suitable		**Q20** *A* significance
Q9 *E* resoluteness		**Q21** *C* evidence
Q10 *D* rude		**Q22** *C* acclimatise
Q11 *A* delighted		**Q23** *B* saunter
Q12 *E* amiable		**Q24** *A* transcribe

Non-Verbal Reasoning

Q1 C

Rotation 90 degrees clockwise, identical diagonal stripes change to vertical.

Q2 C

Reflection in vertical line, becomes smaller and colour changes to vertical stripes

Q3 B

Count increasing so missing shape must have 8 lines

Q4 C

Triangle count increases, building on last pattern, 1 + sign randomly positioned

Q5 A

Circle shading is diagonally arranged from bottom left to top right. Outer triangle shading on middle two columns is alternating between vertical and horizontal

Q6 A

Completes the star image

Q7 C

Reflection in vertical line, ensuring layering is correct with black dot on top of zigzag. Black dot should be the closest part of the image to the reflection line.

Q8 D

Arrow should be closest to the reflection line, and pointing to the right, and must ensure correct position of circle.

Q9 C

Reflection in vertical line, vertical line could be either side

Q10 B

Reflection in vertical line, vertical line could be either side

Q11 D

Reflection in horizontal line, horizontal line could be above or below

Q12 E

Reflection in horizontal line, horizontal line could be above or below

Q13 D

Reflection in vertical line, vertical line could be either side, diagonal stripes into the right angle corner of triangle; circle on base of arrow

Answers to Test A Paper 2

Problem Solving

Q1 I

£6.80

4 × 40 + 8 × 20 = 320p, so

1000 − 320 = 680 pence − £6.80

Q2 B

20p

As the only difference in total cost in the 2 equations is caused by the additional banana (5 up from 4) which must therefore cost 20 pence.

Q3 A

40p

3 pots would be £3.60 without the offer (so £1.20 each), but with the offer, the 3 pots cost only £2.40 (so only 80p each). So the offer saves 40p per pot.

Q4 D

45 minutes

10:45 to 12:30 is 1 hour and 45 minutes or 105 minutes. Shopping takes Harji 55 minutes which leaves 50 minutes wait, but this is reduced by 5 minutes as her friend arrives 5 minutes early.

Q5 G

50 minutes

The frozen food is in her trolley for 20 minutes (5 + 15), and the time to get home is 30 minutes, giving a total of 50 minutes. Time to get home is worked out as follows: her speed is 40 km per hour, so to travel a distance of 20 km will only take $\frac{1}{2}$ an hour or 30 minutes.

Q6 F
240, 420 – 180 = 240

Q7 E
19,200
As 4 tiles will fit in each square metre, and there are 80 × 60 square metres to cover (80 × 60 = 4800) 4 × 4800 = 19 200 tiles

Q8 J
£3.20
Each lemon costs 140p divided by 7 = 20p, so 16 lemons cost 16 × 20 = 320p or £3.20

Q9 C
100 as 140 ÷ 7 × 5 = 100

Q10 H
30p
As the expected change was £130.00 − £123.27 = £6.73 so Harji received 30p less than she should have received.

Cloze

Q1	**E** aspire		**Q11**	**B** ancient
Q2	**C** competitive		**Q12**	**A** empire
Q3	**B** properties		**Q13**	**C** turbulent
Q4	**D** multitude		**Q14**	**D** theatre
Q5	**I** external		**Q15**	**G** spectators
Q6	**F** description		**Q16**	**J** Italy
Q7	**J** exemplified		**Q17**	**F** understood
Q8	**H** stylish		**Q18**	**E** collapsed
Q9	**G** extended		**Q19**	**I** buildings
Q10	**A** parking		**Q20**	**H** survive

Non-Verbal Reasoning

Q1 C
As this is the only 5-sided shape.

Q2 E
As this is the only 5-sided white shape with a 1-sided shape inside.

Q3 B
As this is the only image with an arrow coming from within a 1-sided shape, with another arrow crossing it horizontally.

Q4 D
As the arrow on the bottom of the net turns upside down when the face joins the striped face.

Q5 E
As there is a blank face beneath the heart, and the other blank face wraps around from the left to join the right side of the heart.

Q6 B
As the blank face on the right wraps around to join the left of the pentagon. The net is rotated a half turn to create the pattern displayed on the cube.

Q7 E
As the point of the hexagon will point into the stripes when these faces join. The net is rotated a half turn to create the pattern displayed on the cube, with the blank face ending up on the right side of the cube.

Q8 D
As the point of the hexagon will point into the stripes when these faces join. The net is rotated a quarter turn anti-clockwise to create the pattern displayed on the cube, with the blank face ending up on the top of the cube. E is not possible because the blank face would appear on the left of the cube if the hexagon is on the front face.

Q9 A
AF as the first letter relates to the top shape, and the second letter relates to the direction of the stripes.

Q10 D
BF as the first letter relates to the bottom shape (or top shape), and the second letter relates to the boldness of the line (fine, medium or heavy bold) on the top shape.

Q11 B
AZ as the first letter relates to the shape on the base of the arrow, and the second letter relates to the lower shape.

Q12 E
DZ as the first letter relates to the colour of the top shape, and the second letter relates to the lower shape.

Q13 E
CS as the first letter relates to the shade and stripes on the top shape, and the second letter relates to the shape on top.

Q14 *A*

CR as the first letter relates to the stripes on the top shape, and the second letter relates to whether the arrow head is within or outside the lower shape (or non-existent).

Q15 *C*

DT as the first letter relates to the number of sides on the non 3-dimensional shape, and the second letter relates to the position of the 3-dimensional shape.

Grammar

Q1 *E* sow
Q2 *B* bow
Q3 *B* im
Q4 *A* committee
Q5 *C* curiosity
Q6 *A* dilemma
Q7 *E* existence
Q8 *A* further

Antonyms

Q1 *A* inaudible
Q2 *D* tiny
Q3 *C* unjust
Q4 *A* condemn
Q5 *B* industrious
Q6 *A* inessential
Q7 *D* follower
Q8 *C* admiration
Q9 *A* allow
Q10 *D* disobedient
Q11 *A* imprudent
Q12 *E* noticeable
Q13 *C* folly
Q14 *A* auspicious
Q15 *D* use

Numeracy

Q1 26

Half of 52

Q2 64

Using BODMAS $2 \times 2 = 4$, then add 60

Q3 13

There are two alternating sequences.

Q4 48

This is not exactly divisible by 5, as it would leave a remainder of 3.

Q5 5

Convert $\frac{2}{3}$ into $\frac{4}{6}$ and add the other $\frac{1}{6}$

Q6 5

0.2 is the same as $\frac{2}{10}$ which can be simplified to $\frac{1}{5}$

Q7 59

As this is rounded to 0.59 to 2 significant figures

Q8 0 9.95 rounded to 1 decimal place is 10.0, and 10.0 – 10 = 0

Q9 *B*

360

This is not exactly divisible by 50, it would leave a remainder of 10

Q10 *E*

5

As the radius is half of the diameter of a circle (centre to edge)

Q11 *D*

25.7 cm

Circumference is $2 \times 3.14 \times 5 = 31.4$
Half of this is 15.7. Adding 10 (straight edge) gives 25.7

Q12 *C*

4.9

As mean is the average found by dividing the sum of the data by the number of pieces of data $= \frac{49}{10} = 4.9$

Q13 *D*

0.5P

The first person eats 2 slices, so 3 slices out of 6 will remain, or $\frac{1}{2} = 0.5$ as a decimal

Q14 *D*

6 in 6

As the lowest score on the second dice is 1, giving a total on the two dice of 4 or more

Q15 *A*

(7,6)

As the distance from the start to the end of the first line is (4,6). Add this to (3,0) to give the end coordinates of the second line.

Q16 *A*

$\frac{1}{7}$

Multiplying the top line gives 2, and bottom line 14, and $\frac{2}{14}$ simplifies to $\frac{1}{7}$

Q17 *C*

$\frac{1}{2}$

Multiplying the top line gives 24, and bottom line 48, and $\frac{24}{48}$ simplifies to $\frac{1}{2}$

Q18 *A*

1, as dividing by $\frac{1}{3}$ is the same as multiplying by 3. When multiplying $\frac{3}{9}$ by 3 gives $\frac{9}{9}$ which is the same as 1.

Answers to Test B Paper 1

Comprehension

1. **B**
   Less impressive
2. **E**
   Passage does not say
3. **D**
   Colourful clothes and luxurious hotels
4. **C**
   She removed it on her own.
5. **E**
   Occurring for a long period of time
6. **B**
   Noun
7. **E**
   Due to a family member being ill
8. **D**
   Due to it being the place where her family spent their time
9. **B**
   A design secret
10. **E**
    Grey and blue tones

Shuffled Sentences

1. **C**
   engine *The boy enjoyed sitting in his car which he had bought that morning.*
2. **D**
   awful *Despite eating her last biscuit the girl was still hungry.*
3. **B**
   brand *We like listening to the radio show which plays classical music.*
4. **E**
   extend *As a result of his training the young man became a talented dancer.*
5. **A**
   courageous *According to most people gardening is good exercise.*
6. **C**
   quietly *The competition started promptly at ten o'clock despite the thunderstorm overhead.*
7. **E**
   house *He finally completed reading the lengthy novel.*

The word 'and' does not appear in the shuffled sentence and can be eliminated immediately.

8. **B**
   severe *According to some scientists eggs are good for you in many ways.*
9. **D**
   flossed *All dentists recommend brushing your teeth twice a day.*
10. **A**
    chargeable *The singers were amazing and the atmosphere was electric.*
11. **C**
    heavily *Although I have been to the supermarket today I have still run out of milk.*
12. **A**
    arranged *The interior designer has produced an attractive sketch.*
    The words 'of' and 'house' do not appear in the shuffled sentence and can be eliminated immediately.
13. **E**
    standard *We were not looking forward to our aunt's party but we had a wonderful time.*
14. **D**
    threw *Most of the neighbours were awoken by the dog barking.*
15. **A**
    calm *The overgrown grass in the garden needs mowing.*
    The word 'for' does not appear in the shuffled sentence and can be eliminated immediately.

Numeracy

1. *28*
   2015 is not a leap year as it is odd, so 25 + 2 + 1 (includes both the 3rd Feb and 2nd March)
   1 relates to the 3rd of February in addition as the question is inclusive dates.
2. *8*
   56 divided by 7
3. *19*
   $b + 2b + 3b = 6b$, so $6b + 1 =$ perimeter.
   As the question tells us $b = 3$, $(6 \times 3) + 1 = 19$
4. *12*
   As you are walking at 2.5 miles in each hour (or 60 minutes). A distance of 0.5 miles is one fifth of 2.5 miles. So, if 2.5 miles are covered

in 60 minutes, one fifth of the distance would be covered in one fifth of the time. 60 divided by 5 is 12 minutes.

5. *10*

as Jenny will always be 2 years younger than Kate.

6. *6*

as the difference is halving between each consecutive pair of numbers in the sequence. Differences are 16, 8, 4 so the next difference is 2.

7. *20*

as each term is 5 less than the previous term. To work out the 18th (or any term in the sequence) use $110 - 5n$ where n is the position of the term wanted (18 in this case). $110 - (5 \times 18) = 20$

8. *28*

as this is 84 divided by 3 (the tank is one third empty).

9. *7*

as 1.5 l equals 1,500 ml, and when this is divided by 200, the answer is 7 full cups with a remainder of 100 ml.

10. *12*

180 divided by 15 (as quarter of an hour is 15 minutes).

11. *6*

The vertices are the corners on this 3D shape, and there are 3 on each triangle at the ends of the prism.

12. *34*

Using BODMAS to first calculate the brackets which come to 26, then add 8.

13. *88*

Problem Solving

1. **G**

12 days as half the men will take twice as long to fit.

2. **C**

24 (6 × 4)

3. **B**

3, as 4 tiles fit into each metre squared, so 4 × 24 = 96 tiles required. 40 tiles per box (2 boxes have only 80, so 3 boxes will be required).

4. **I**

£150 (0.25 × £600)

5. **F**

£1,200 as 1% of £20,000 is £200, so 6% is 6 × 200 = £1,200

6. **A**

£450, as the sale price is $\frac{2}{3}$ of the original price.

7. **J**

52 weeks in a year divided by 4 = 13 weeks.

8. **H**

£1,100 (21,100 − 20,000)

9. **D**

£28,900 (increase in house value of £50,000 less the cost of the new kitchen of £21,100)

10. **E**

£25,000 (£250,000 divided by 10)

Synonyms

1. **C** insignificant		13. **A** alliance
2. **B** arc		14. **C** details
3. **D** setback		15. **B** unconventional
4. **E** ineffective		16. **C** acrimonious
5. **A** cliff		17. **A** blend
6. **E** anguish		18. **E** ultimate
7. **C** upright		19. **A** thrive
8. **C** exterior		20. **A** indifferent
9. **E** slender		21. **E** mode
10. **B** gap		22. **C** parade
11. **C** curious		23. **A** projection
12. **D** accomplished		

Non-Verbal Reasoning

Q1. **E**

Sequence shapes repeat after 3 images in same order. The arrows are rotating clockwise.

Q2. **B**

Sequence shapes repeat after 3 images in same order. The arrows are rotating clockwise.

Q3. **D**

Sequence shapes alternate in both shading and number of sides. The arch switches from top to bottom and also from shaded to blank. The arch is always blank when beneath the hexagon.

Q4. **C**

Sequence shapes alternate in both shading and number of sides. The arch switches from top to bottom and also from shaded to blank. The pentagon also turns a half turn from one image to the next.

Q5. **E**

All shapes are grey and the number of sides in the sequence increases by one each time (it is necessary to add the number of sides where there is more than one shape). 3 sides on the triangle + 1 side on each of the 2 circles gives 5 sides.

Q6. C

All shapes are grey and the number of sides in the sequence increases by one each time (it is necessary to add the number of sides where there is more than one shape). 5 sides on the pentagon + 4 sides on square gives 9 sides.

Q7. C

Background shapes large, whilst foreground shape smaller. Also both large and small shapes switch shading as the sequence continues. The number of sides of the shapes is irrelevant.

Q8. B

Background shapes large, whilst foreground shape smaller. Also both large and small shapes switch shading as the sequence continues. The number of sides of the shapes is irrelevant.

Q9. D

Triangles swap from equilateral (having two, four point stars and a horizontal line underneath), to right angled (having an arrow underneath and one black, four-point star).

Q10. E

Triangles swap from equilateral (having two, four point stars and a horizontal line underneath), to right angled (having an arrow underneath and one black, four-point star).

Q11. E

Triangles swap from grey equilateral (having a left facing arrow underneath), to white right angled (having a right facing arrow underneath). Number of stars decrease from 3 to 2 to 1 but with 5-point stars for second half of sequence.

Q12. C

Triangles swap from grey equilateral (having a left facing arrow underneath), to white right angled (having a right facing arrow underneath). Number of stars decrease from 3 to 2 to 1 but with 5-point stars for second half of sequence.

Q13. C

Circles on top alternate black and white, whilst arrows switch direction beneath and stripes change from vertical to horizontal. First 3 arrows are double headed, second 3 are single headed.

Q14. D

Circles on top alternate black and white, whilst arrows switch direction beneath and stripes change from vertical to horizontal. First 3 arrows are double headed, second 3 are single headed.

Answers to Test B Paper 2

Problem Solving

1. I

£550 for each of the child tickets. The adult tickets were £1,100 each. Effectively, the two child tickets cost the same as one adult flight. £3,300 ÷ 3 = £1,100 per adult, and half of this for each child.

2. D

17:00 Flight leaves Singapore 3 hours later at 10:00. Add 5 hours flight time to Sydney, and add 2 hours to reflect the time difference.

3. J

10 : 8 + 2

4. B

06:00 Flight scheduled to take off at 9 a.m. 3 hours earlier is 6 a.m.

5. F

05:00 as this is 1 hour before check-in opens.

6. H

£1,100 : $1,925 divided by 1.75 = 1,100. It may be easier to convert 1.75 into an improper fraction $\left(\frac{7}{4}\right)$. Dividing by $\frac{7}{4}$ is done by multiplying by $\frac{4}{7}$.

1925 × 4 = 7,700. Divide this by 7 to give £1,100.

7. A

£500 : $875 divided by $\frac{7}{4}$ (or 1.75) is the same as multiplying by 4 then dividing by 7.

4 x 875 = 3,500

3500 ÷ 7 = £500

8. G

£20 : 50% of $70 = $35

$35 divided by 1.75 = £20

9. C

8: 468 − 15 = 453

461 − 453 = 8 people boarded initially in Singapore.

10. J

10: 2015 − 2005 = 10 years (the flight took off in London on 21 December 2015, and the holiday was only a 2-week holiday, so the closest answer is 10 years).

Cloze

1. **G** advertisement
2. **A** forming
3. **C** technical
4. **J** remote
5. **F** apparent
6. **B** unearthed
7. **E** carefully
8. **H** graveyard
9. **I** guided
10. **D** visiting
11. **I** travelling
12. **J** motorists
13. **G** breakdown
14. **A** provisions
15. **E** reputable
16. **F** tow
17. **B** treacherous
18. **H** estimated
19. **D** working
20. **C** necessary

Non-Verbal Reasoning

1. D

Only answer without a star (all others have stars).

2. B

Only answer with 4 shapes (all others have 3).

3. E

Only answer where the grey shapes are not a reflection of each other in a horizontal line.

4. D

Only answer where the shapes are not the same.

5. A

Only answer where the number of rectangles is not even.

6. B

Only image where both arrows come from the same side.

7. A

Net requires half-turn rotation

8. B

No rotation of net required

9. E

No rotation of net required

10. C

Net requires half-turn rotation

11. C

No rotation of net required

12. D

No rotation of net required

13. A

Net requires half-turn rotation

Antonyms

1. **C** apathetic
2. **A** barren
3. **B** unreliable
4. **E** hide
5. **C** embrace
6. **B** dispute
7. **B** divide
8. **C** fertile
9. **B** original
10. **E** combined
11. **B** cheer
12. **C** purify
13. **E** bland
14. **B** experienced
15. **B** upgrade

Numeracy

1. 99

2. 11

Left-hand side equals 33, so 11 must be missing number (as $33 = 11 \times 3$).

3. 22

as the difference between each pair of consecutive numbers is increasing by 1. Differences are 1, 2, 3, 4 so next is 5 and $17 + 5 = 22$.

4. 8

as adding 3 back on to 61 means 64 is 8 times the number, so the number must be 8.

5. 27

This is the addition of all numbers within those sets (exclude 3 outside of all sets) $7 + 5 + 4 + 5 + 6 = 27$.

6. 30

7. 7

8. 8

Highest less lowest is $9 − 1 = 8$.

9. £80

as £64 is now 80% of the original price. Divide this by 4 and multiply that by 5 to scale the amount back up to the original price. $64 ÷ 4 = 16$, and $16 \times 5 = 80$.

10. *7*

Rearrange by adding y to both sides to give
21 = 3y, so y = 21 divided by 3 = 7.

11. *56*

Write all numbers of cards as an expression
of one of the other people in the question, e.g.
Say Martin has y cards, therefore Judy has 2y
cards (as she has twice as many), and Jay will
have 6y cards. Total cards could be written as 9y
and this equals 252 cards, so y = 252 ÷ 9 = 28,
and so Judy has 28 × 2 = 56 cards.

12. *13*

13. *18*

6 pieces in each of the 3 cakes.

14. *7*

Coins would be £2, 50p, 20p, 10p, 5p, 2p, 2p.

15. *56*

(8 × 7)

16. *8*

17. *7*

Half of 14

18. *1*

as in 5 years my mother will be 45, and
my older sister will be a third of 45 which
is 15. So if my sister will be 15 in 5 years'
time, that means she is 10 now. I am 9 years
younger which means I am 10 − 9 = 1
year old.

Pupil's Full Name:

Instructions:
Mark the boxes correctly like this ✏

Please sign your name here:

Comprehension

Example 1

★   B   C   D   E

Practice Question 1

A   B   C   D   E

#					
1	A	B	C	D	E
2	A	B	C	D	E
3	A	B	C	D	E
4	A	B	C	D	E
5	A	B	C	D	E
6	A	B	C	D	E
7	A	B	C	D	E
8	A	B	C	D	E
9	A	B	C	D	E
10	A	B	C	D	E

Shuffled Sentences

Example 1

★   B   C   D   E

Practice Question 1

A   B   C   D   E

#					
1	A	B	C	D	E
2	A	B	C	D	E
3	A	B	C	D	E
4	A	B	C	D	E
5	A	B	C	D	E
6	A	B	C	D	E
7	A	B	C	D	E
8	A	B	C	D	E
9	A	B	C	D	E
10	A	B	C	D	E
11	A	B	C	D	E
12	A	B	C	D	E
13	A	B	C	D	E
14	A	B	C	D	E
15	A	B	C	D	E

Numeracy

Example — 3 7 (3 and 7 marked)

Practice Question 1

1

2

Each answer grid has two columns with digits 0–9.

3, **4**, **5**, **6**

7, **8**, **9**, **10**

11, **12**, **13**

Problem Solving

Example 1

    A   B   C   D   E

Practice Question 1

    A   B   C   D   E

1 A B C D E
2 A B C D E
3 A B C D E
4 A B C D E
5 A B C D E
6 A B C D E
7 A B C D E
8 A B C D E
9 A B C D E
10 A B C D E

Synonyms

Example 1

    A   B   C   D   E

Practice Question 1

    A   B   C   D   E

1 A B C D E
2 A B C D E
3 A B C D E
4 A B C D E
5 A B C D E
6 A B C D E
7 A B C D E
8 A B C D E
9 A B C D E
10 A B C D E
11 A B C D E
12 A B C D E
13 A B C D E
14 A B C D E
15 A B C D E
16 A B C D E
17 A B C D E
18 A B C D E
19 A B C D E
20 A B C D E
21 A B C D E

22 A B C D E
23 A B C D E
24 A B C D E

Non-Verbal Reasoning

REFLECTION Example 1

    A   B   C   D   E

REFLECTION Practice Question 1

    A   B   C   D   E

CONNECTION Example 2

    A   B   C   D   E

CONNECTION Practice Question 2

    A   B   C   D   E

1 A B C D E
2 A B C D E
3 A B C D E
4 A B C D E
5 A B C D E
6 A B C D E
7 A B C D E
8 A B C D E
9 A B C D E
10 A B C D E
11 A B C D E
12 A B C D E
13 A B C D E

Pupil's Full Name:

2

Instructions:
Mark the boxes correctly like this ⬛

Please sign your name here:

Problem Solving

Example 1

Ⓐ Ⓑ Ⓒ Ⓓ Ⓔ Ⓕ Ⓖ Ⓗ Ⓘ Ⓙ

Practice Question 1

Ⓐ Ⓑ Ⓒ Ⓓ Ⓔ Ⓕ Ⓖ Ⓗ Ⓘ Ⓙ

1 Ⓐ Ⓑ Ⓒ Ⓓ Ⓔ Ⓕ Ⓖ Ⓗ Ⓘ Ⓙ
2 Ⓐ Ⓑ Ⓒ Ⓓ Ⓔ Ⓕ Ⓖ Ⓗ Ⓘ Ⓙ
3 Ⓐ Ⓑ Ⓒ Ⓓ Ⓔ Ⓕ Ⓖ Ⓗ Ⓘ Ⓙ
4 Ⓐ Ⓑ Ⓒ Ⓓ Ⓔ Ⓕ Ⓖ Ⓗ Ⓘ Ⓙ
5 Ⓐ Ⓑ Ⓒ Ⓓ Ⓔ Ⓕ Ⓖ Ⓗ Ⓘ Ⓙ
6 Ⓐ Ⓑ Ⓒ Ⓓ Ⓔ Ⓕ Ⓖ Ⓗ Ⓘ Ⓙ
7 Ⓐ Ⓑ Ⓒ Ⓓ Ⓔ Ⓕ Ⓖ Ⓗ Ⓘ Ⓙ
8 Ⓐ Ⓑ Ⓒ Ⓓ Ⓔ Ⓕ Ⓖ Ⓗ Ⓘ Ⓙ
9 Ⓐ Ⓑ Ⓒ Ⓓ Ⓔ Ⓕ Ⓖ Ⓗ Ⓘ Ⓙ
10 Ⓐ Ⓑ Ⓒ Ⓓ Ⓔ Ⓕ Ⓖ Ⓗ Ⓘ Ⓙ

Cloze

Example 1

Ⓐ Ⓑ Ⓒ Ⓓ Ⓔ

Practice Question 1

Ⓐ Ⓑ Ⓒ Ⓓ Ⓔ

1 Ⓐ Ⓑ Ⓒ Ⓓ Ⓔ Ⓕ Ⓖ Ⓗ Ⓘ Ⓙ
2 Ⓐ Ⓑ Ⓒ Ⓓ Ⓔ Ⓕ Ⓖ Ⓗ Ⓘ Ⓙ
3 Ⓐ Ⓑ Ⓒ Ⓓ Ⓔ Ⓕ Ⓖ Ⓗ Ⓘ Ⓙ
4 Ⓐ Ⓑ Ⓒ Ⓓ Ⓔ Ⓕ Ⓖ Ⓗ Ⓘ Ⓙ
5 Ⓐ Ⓑ Ⓒ Ⓓ Ⓔ Ⓕ Ⓖ Ⓗ Ⓘ Ⓙ
6 Ⓐ Ⓑ Ⓒ Ⓓ Ⓔ Ⓕ Ⓖ Ⓗ Ⓘ Ⓙ
7 Ⓐ Ⓑ Ⓒ Ⓓ Ⓔ Ⓕ Ⓖ Ⓗ Ⓘ Ⓙ
8 Ⓐ Ⓑ Ⓒ Ⓓ Ⓔ Ⓕ Ⓖ Ⓗ Ⓘ Ⓙ
9 Ⓐ Ⓑ Ⓒ Ⓓ Ⓔ Ⓕ Ⓖ Ⓗ Ⓘ Ⓙ
10 Ⓐ Ⓑ Ⓒ Ⓓ Ⓔ Ⓕ Ⓖ Ⓗ Ⓘ Ⓙ
11 Ⓐ Ⓑ Ⓒ Ⓓ Ⓔ Ⓕ Ⓖ Ⓗ Ⓘ Ⓙ
12 Ⓐ Ⓑ Ⓒ Ⓓ Ⓔ Ⓕ Ⓖ Ⓗ Ⓘ Ⓙ
13 Ⓐ Ⓑ Ⓒ Ⓓ Ⓔ Ⓕ Ⓖ Ⓗ Ⓘ Ⓙ
14 Ⓐ Ⓑ Ⓒ Ⓓ Ⓔ Ⓕ Ⓖ Ⓗ Ⓘ Ⓙ

15 Ⓐ Ⓑ Ⓒ Ⓓ Ⓔ Ⓕ Ⓖ Ⓗ Ⓘ Ⓙ
16 Ⓐ Ⓑ Ⓒ Ⓓ Ⓔ Ⓕ Ⓖ Ⓗ Ⓘ Ⓙ
17 Ⓐ Ⓑ Ⓒ Ⓓ Ⓔ Ⓕ Ⓖ Ⓗ Ⓘ Ⓙ
18 Ⓐ Ⓑ Ⓒ Ⓓ Ⓔ Ⓕ Ⓖ Ⓗ Ⓘ Ⓙ
19 Ⓐ Ⓑ Ⓒ Ⓓ Ⓔ Ⓕ Ⓖ Ⓗ Ⓘ Ⓙ
20 Ⓐ Ⓑ Ⓒ Ⓓ Ⓔ Ⓕ Ⓖ Ⓗ Ⓘ Ⓙ

Non-Verbal Reasoning

CUBES Example 1

Ⓐ Ⓑ Ⓒ Ⓓ Ⓔ

CUBES Practice Question 1

Ⓐ Ⓑ Ⓒ Ⓓ Ⓔ

BELONGS TO GROUP Example 2

Ⓐ Ⓑ Ⓒ Ⓓ Ⓔ

BELONGS TO GROUP
Practice Question 2

Ⓐ Ⓑ Ⓒ Ⓓ Ⓔ

1 Ⓐ Ⓑ Ⓒ Ⓓ Ⓔ
2 Ⓐ Ⓑ Ⓒ Ⓓ Ⓔ
3 Ⓐ Ⓑ Ⓒ Ⓓ Ⓔ
4 Ⓐ Ⓑ Ⓒ Ⓓ Ⓔ
5 Ⓐ Ⓑ Ⓒ Ⓓ Ⓔ
6 Ⓐ Ⓑ Ⓒ Ⓓ Ⓔ
7 Ⓐ Ⓑ Ⓒ Ⓓ Ⓔ
8 Ⓐ Ⓑ Ⓒ Ⓓ Ⓔ
9 Ⓐ Ⓑ Ⓒ Ⓓ Ⓔ
10 Ⓐ Ⓑ Ⓒ Ⓓ Ⓔ
11 Ⓐ Ⓑ Ⓒ Ⓓ Ⓔ
12 Ⓐ Ⓑ Ⓒ Ⓓ Ⓔ
13 Ⓐ Ⓑ Ⓒ Ⓓ Ⓔ
14 Ⓐ Ⓑ Ⓒ Ⓓ Ⓔ
15 Ⓐ Ⓑ Ⓒ Ⓓ Ⓔ

Grammar

Example 1

A   B   **C**   D   E

Practice Question 1

A   B   C   D   E

1 A B C D E
2 A B C D E
3 A B C D E
4 A B C D E
5 A B C D E
6 A B C D E
7 A B C D E
8 A B C D E

Antonyms

Example 1

A   B   C   D   E

Practice Question 1

A   B   C   D   E

1 A B C D E
2 A B C D E
3 A B C D E
4 A B C D E
5 A B C D E
6 A B C D E
7 A B C D E
8 A B C D E
9 A B C D E
10 A B C D E
11 A B C D E
12 A B C D E
13 A B C D E
14 A B C D E
15 A B C D E

Numeracy

Example: 3 7

Practice Question 1, **1**, **2** — digit grids (0–9)

3, **4**, **5**, **6** — digit grids (0–9)

7, **8** — digit grids (0–9)

9 A B C D E
10 A B C D E
11 A B C D E
12 A B C D E
13 A B C D E
14 A B C D E
15 A B C D E
16 A B C D E
17 A B C D E
18 A B C D E

Pupil's Full Name:

Instructions:
Mark the boxes correctly like this ▬

Please sign your name here:

Comprehension

Example 1

A ▬   B   C   D   E

Practice Question 1

A   B   C   D   E

1   A   B   C   D   E
2   A   B   C   D   E
3   A   B   C   D   E
4   A   B   C   D   E
5   A   B   C   D   E
6   A   B   C   D   E
7   A   B   C   D   E
8   A   B   C   D   E
9   A   B   C   D   E
10 A   B   C   D   E

Shuffled Sentences

Example 1

A ▬   B   C   D   E

Practice Question 1

A   B   C   D   E

1   A   B   C   D   E
2   A   B   C   D   E
3   A   B   C   D   E
4   A   B   C   D   E
5   A   B   C   D   E
6   A   B   C   D   E
7   A   B   C   D   E
8   A   B   C   D   E
9   A   B   C   D   E
10 A   B   C   D   E
11 A   B   C   D   E
12 A   B   C   D   E
13 A   B   C   D   E
14 A   B   C   D   E
15 A   B   C   D   E

Numeracy

Example 3 7

Practice Question 1

1   2

0 0	0 0	0 0	0 0
1 1	1 1	1 1	1 1
2 2	2 2	2 2	2 2
3̶ 3	3 3	3 3	3 3
4 4	4 4	4 4	4 4
5 5	5 5	5 5	5 5
6 6	6 6	6 6	6 6
7 7̶	7 7	7 7	7 7
8 8	8 8	8 8	8 8
9 9	9 9	9 9	9 9

3   4   5   6

0 0	0 0	0 0	0 0
1 1	1 1	1 1	1 1
2 2	2 2	2 2	2 2
3 3	3 3	3 3	3 3
4 4	4 4	4 4	4 4
5 5	5 5	5 5	5 5
6 6	6 6	6 6	6 6
7 7	7 7	7 7	7 7
8 8	8 8	8 8	8 8
9 9	9 9	9 9	9 9

7   8   9   10

0 0	0 0	0 0	0 0
1 1	1 1	1 1	1 1
2 2	2 2	2 2	2 2
3 3	3 3	3 3	3 3
4 4	4 4	4 4	4 4
5 5	5 5	5 5	5 5
6 6	6 6	6 6	6 6
7 7	7 7	7 7	7 7
8 8	8 8	8 8	8 8
9 9	9 9	9 9	9 9

11   12   13

0 0	0 0	0 0
1 1	1 1	1 1
2 2	2 2	2 2
3 3	3 3	3 3
4 4	4 4	4 4
5 5	5 5	5 5
6 6	6 6	6 6
7 7	7 7	7 7
8 8	8 8	8 8
9 9	9 9	9 9

Problem Solving

Example 1

A B C D E F G H I J

Practice Question 1

A B C D E F G H I J

1 A B C D E F G H I J
2 A B C D E F G H I J
3 A B C D E F G H I J
4 A B C D E F G H I J
5 A B C D E F G H I J
6 A B C D E F G H I J
7 A B C D E F G H I J
8 A B C D E F G H I J
9 A B C D E F G H I J
10 A B C D E F G H I J

Synonyms

Example 1

A B C D E

Practice Question 1

A B C D E

1 A B C D E
2 A B C D E
3 A B C D E
4 A B C D E
5 A B C D E
6 A B C D E
7 A B C D E
8 A B C D E
9 A B C D E
10 A B C D E
11 A B C D E
12 A B C D E
13 A B C D E
14 A B C D E
15 A B C D E
16 A B C D E
17 A B C D E
18 A B C D E
19 A B C D E
20 A B C D E
21 A B C D E

22 A B C D E
23 A B C D E

Non-Verbal Reasoning

COMPLETE THE SEQUENCE
Example 1

A B C D E

COMPLETE THE SEQUENCE
Practice Question 1

A B C D E

1 A B C D E
2 A B C D E
3 A B C D E
4 A B C D E
5 A B C D E
6 A B C D E
7 A B C D E
8 A B C D E
9 A B C D E
10 A B C D E
11 A B C D E
12 A B C D E
13 A B C D E
14 A B C D E

Pupil's Full Name:

2

Instructions:
Mark the boxes correctly like this ▰

Please sign your name here:

Problem Solving

Example 1

▰ B C D E F G H I J

Practice Question 1

A B C D E F G H I J

1 A B C D E F G H I J
2 A B C D E F G H I J
3 A B C D E F G H I J
4 A B C D E F G H I J
5 A B C D E F G H I J
6 A B C D E F G H I J
7 A B C D E F G H I J
8 A B C D E F G H I J
9 A B C D E F G H I J
10 A B C D E F G H I J

Cloze

Example 1

▰ B C D E F G H I J

Practice Question 1

A B C D E F G H I J

1 A B C D E F G H I J
2 A B C D E F G H I J
3 A B C D E F G H I J
4 A B C D E F G H I J
5 A B C D E F G H I J
6 A B C D E F G H I J
7 A B C D E F G H I J
8 A B C D E F G H I J
9 A B C D E F G H I J
10 A B C D E F G H I J
11 A B C D E F G H I J
12 A B C D E F G H I J
13 A B C D E F G H I J
14 A B C D E F G H I J

15 A B C D E F G H I J
16 A B C D E F G H I J
17 A B C D E F G H I J
18 A B C D E F G H I J
19 A B C D E F G H I J
20 A B C D E F G H I J

Non-Verbal Reasoning

CUBE NET Example 1

A B C D ▰

CUBE NET Practice Question 1

A B C D E

LEAST SIMILAR Example 2

A ▰ C D E

LEAST SIMILAR Practice Question 2

A B C D E

1 A B C D E
2 A B C D E
3 A B C D E
4 A B C D E
5 A B C D E
6 A B C D E
7 A B C D E
8 A B C D E
9 A B C D E
10 A B C D E
11 A B C D E
12 A B C D E
13 A B C D E

Antonyms

Example 1

    A   B   C   D   E

Practice Question 1

    A   B   C   D   E

1 A B C D E
2 A B C D E
3 A B C D E
4 A B C D E
5 A B C D E
6 A B C D E
7 A B C D E
8 A B C D E
9 A B C D E
10 A B C D E
11 A B C D E
12 A B C D E
13 A B C D E
14 A B C D E
15 A B C D E

Numeracy

Example   **Practice**   **1**   **2**

3 7   **Question 1**

(Numeracy answer grids with digits 0–9 for Example, Practice Question 1, 1, 2, 3, 4, 5, 6)

(Numeracy answer grids with digits 0–9 for questions 7, 8, 9, 10, 11, 12, 13, 14, 15, 16, 17, 18)

In partnership with

11+
Success

CEM Tests

Practice Test Papers

Book 2

4 test papers,
plus audio download

Philip
McMahon

Contents

Guidance notes for parents

What your child will need to sit these papers

- A quiet place to sit the exam
- A clock which is visible to your child
- A way to play the audio download
- A pencil and an eraser
- A piece of paper

Your child should not use a calculator for any of these papers.

How to invigilate the test papers

Your child should sit Test C, Paper 1 then have a 15-minute break. They should then sit Paper 2. Don't help your child or allow any talking. Review the answers with your child and help improve their weaker areas. At a later date, your child should sit Test D, Papers 1 and 2 in a two-hour session.

Step 1: Cut out the answers and keep them hidden from your child.

Step 2: Tear out the answer sheet section. Your child should write their full name on top of the first answer sheet. Give them the question paper booklet. They must not open the paper until they are told to do so by the audio instructions.

Step 3: Start the audio.

Step 4: Ask your child to work through the practice questions before the time starts for each section. An example is already marked on each section of the answer sheet. Your child should mark the answer sheet clearly and check that the practice questions are correctly marked.

Step 5: Mark the answer sheet. Then, together with your child, work through the questions that were answered incorrectly. When working through the Non-verbal Reasoning sections, ensure you have the question papers open to help explain the answers to your child.

How your child should complete the answer sheet

Your child MUST NOT write their answers on the question paper, they must use the answer sheet. They should put a horizontal line through the boxes on the answer sheet. To change an answer, your child should fully erase the incorrect answer and then clearly select a new answer. Any rough workings should be done on a separate piece of paper.

The audio instructions

Both papers have audio instructions to allow your child to learn, listen and act upon audio instructions. Audio instructions are at the start, during and at the end of the sections. Audio warnings on the time remaining will be given at varying intervals. Your child should listen out for these warnings.

The symbols at the foot of the page

Written instructions are at the foot of the page. Your child MUST follow these instructions:

Continue working

Stop and wait for instructions

Your child can review questions within the allocated time, but must not move onto the next section until they are allowed to do so.

The instructions and examples at the beginning of the section

In the instructions, your child should look for: the time allowed; how many questions there are; and how to complete the answers.

Examples are at the beginning of every section to show the type of question included in a particular section. The example questions will be worked through as part of the audio instructions.

Developing time-management skills and working at speed

These test papers have been used with previous pupils of the CEM exam in various counties. They provide essential practice of the types of questions which could arise, in addition to the strictly timed conditions, which will help your child practise their time-management skills.

Marking the papers

Each question is worth one mark.

Scores

Overall scores your child should be aiming for:

- 75% or more on the first pack of 2 papers if taken in the weeks leading up to the exam
- 70% or more on the second pack of 2 papers if taken in the weeks leading up to the exam.

A weighted score attaches a certain amount of weight to each section in the exam.

How to work out your child's score:

Add together the scores for Non-verbal Reasoning and Maths sections (both Numeracy and Problem Solving). This will give you score A. This relates to both sections in all papers.

Then add together the remaining scores for all English sections, which will give you score B.

Then add scores A and B together and divide them by 2.

This will give you an average weighted score across the 2 packs.

To calculate your child's weighted score as a percentage, divide your child's score by the maximum score, and multiply it by 100.

Once you have completed this, you will have two percentages and the combined weighted score across the two papers is the middle of these two percentages.

For example: If your child scores 46 out of 92 for English, this equals 50%.

If your child scores 62 out of 82, this equals approximately 76%. So the combined weighted score across the two papers is 50% + 76%, which equals 126%. If you divide this by 2, this equals 63%. This is your child's weighted score.

The maximum scores:

Test C Paper 1 English – 39

Test C Paper 1 Maths and Non-verbal Reasoning – 48

Test C Paper 2 English – 57

Test C Paper 2 Maths and Non-verbal Reasoning – 25

Test D Paper 1 English – 30

Test D Paper 1 Maths and Non-verbal Reasoning – 43

Test D Paper 2 English – 57

Test D Paper 2 Maths and Non-verbal Reasoning – 25

English maximum scores, Test C Papers 1 and 2 – 96

Maths and Non-verbal Reasoning maximum scores, Test C Papers 1 and 2 – 73

English maximum scores, Test D Papers 1 and 2 – 87

Maths and Non-verbal Reasoning maximum scores, Test D Papers 1 and 2 – 68

Please note the following:

As the content varies from year to year in CEM exams, a good score in this paper does not guarantee a pass, and a lower score may not always suggest a fail!

What happens if your child does not score a good mark?

Identify strengths and weaknesses

Continue to provide a wide variety of questions to build your child's knowledge. Focus on the areas in which your child did not perform as well.

Timings

Allow your child to continue practising working under timed conditions.

Test C Paper 1

Instructions

1. Ensure you have pencils and an eraser with you.

2. Make sure you are able to see a clock or watch.

3. Write your name on the answer sheet.

4. Do not open the question booklet until you are told to do so by the audio instructions.

5. Listen carefully to the audio instructions given.

6. Mark your answers on the answer sheet only.

7. All workings must be completed on a separate piece of paper.

8. You should not use a calculator, dictionary or thesaurus at any point in this paper.

9. Move through the papers as quickly as possible and with care.

10. Follow the instructions at the foot of each page.

11. You should mark your answers with a horizontal strike, as shown on the answer sheet.

12. If you want to change your answer, ensure that you rub out your first answer and that your second answer is clearly more visible.

13. You can go back and review any questions that are within the section you are working on only. You must await further instructions before moving onto another section.

Symbols and Phrases used in the Tests

 Instructions  Time allowed for this section Stop and wait for further instructions Continue working

Comprehension

 YOU HAVE 8 MINUTES TO COMPLETE THE FOLLOWING SECTION.

YOU HAVE 10 QUESTIONS TO COMPLETE WITHIN THE TIME GIVEN.

EXAMPLES

Comprehension Example

Some people choose to start their Christmas shopping early in October. It has been reported that some people even buy their Christmas presents in the sales in August. In recent years, people have the option of purchasing their Christmas presents online.

Example 1

According to the passage, what is the earliest that people start their Christmas shopping?

A   In the preceding summer
B   In the preceding October
C   In the preceding November
D   Christmas Eve
E   In early December

The correct answer is A. This has already been marked in Example 1 in the Comprehension section of your answer sheet.

Practice Question 1

What has caused a change in how people shop, in recent years?

A   There are more shops.
B   Shops are more crowded.
C   You can easily organise your journey to the shops.
D   New products are available
E   There has been a rise in use of the Internet

The correct answer is E. Please mark this in Practice Question 1 in the Comprehension section of your answer sheet.

STOP AND WAIT FOR FURTHER INSTRUCTIONS

The Popularity of Allotments

Line 5

The changing of the seasons can be clearly seen in allotments, which are often located on the periphery of residential areas in Britain. Allotments are pieces of land divided into plots and then allocated to families or individuals. Allotments, which were once left barren, have once again become popular with young people wanting to be self-sufficient, providing the majority of their food for themselves and their young families. They do however, require a significant investment of time and energy.

The winter months are often a period of inactivity. The ground is too hard for much work to happen, and the weather too cold for many crops to grow.

Line 10

Once spring has sprung, the allotments become a hive of activity with everyone attending their plots at least once a fortnight. At this stage in the year, the work is ploughing and sowing the vegetables, which the allotment holders hope will grow in abundance from that point onwards. In a good year, when the conditions are right, there should be a plentiful harvest.

Line 15

Line 20

With the onset of summer, the work changes. Regular watering is needed to ensure that the crops do not wilt and die. There is often an additional peril in the form of insects, which can engulf and devastate the crops. The treatment of these pests depends on the allotment holders' beliefs, as to whether they want to use pesticides or natural, environmentally-friendly alternatives, to defeat an infestation. Traditional methods, such as nets placed over brassicas (purple sprouting broccoli) can ward off butterflies from laying their eggs. If one butterfly lays its eggs here, an entire crop can be destroyed as a result. When the sun is shining the weeds also grow and this means that hoeing is required on a weekly basis.

Line 25

In the autumn months, most of the crops are harvested and enjoyed. Many are cut down in preparation for the following year. Expertise and knowledge of the individual varieties of all the crops are required. An amateur allotment holder needs to learn about sowing, growing and harvesting to ensure a plentiful yield.

Line 30

The waiting lists for allotments are growing year by year as their popularity increases. Allotments are normally held for a generation, resulting in long waiting lists of many years in some places.

(1) Read the passage above and answer the following questions.

In the context of the passage, what type of word is the word 'allocated'?

A Metaphor
B Noun
C Verb
D Homophone
E Adjective

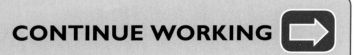
CONTINUE WORKING

(2) According to the passage, which phrase best describes the current situation with allotments?

    A   Allotments are very popular
    B   Nobody wants an allotment
    C   Allotments are very expensive to buy
    D   Allotments are mainly held by older people
    E   Allotments are reversing

(3) According to the passage, which of the following best describes the following phrase:

'a significant investment of time and energy'?

    A   Allotments need power
    B   Allotments are very expensive
    C   Allotments need expertise
    D   Allotments can be bought and sold
    E   Allotments require people to spend time and effort

(4) According to the passage, which phrase best describes what happens in the winter months?

    A   People attend every two weeks
    B   People attend every week
    C   Crops grow well in the winter
    D   Nothing happens
    E   Allotment holders harvest their crops

(5) In the context of the passage, what is the meaning of 'a hive of activity'?

    A   A place where bees live
    B   A busy place
    C   A place which is extremely quiet
    D   A place where people go to be active
    E   A place to have some time alone

(6) What is the meaning of 'abundance'?

    A   A large quantity
    B   A small quantity
    C   A straight line
    D   A regular pattern
    E   A haphazard way

CONTINUE WORKING

(7) Which word is the most similar to 'engulf'?

A   Formulate
B   Harden
C   Arrange
D   Envelop
E   Be aware of

(8) According to the passage, how often should 'hoeing' be completed?

A   Every three weeks
B   Every ten days
C   Once a fortnight
D   Every five days
E   Every seven days

(9) Which word is the most similar to the phrase 'ward off'?

A   Worshipful
B   General
C   Aggregate
D   Repel
E   Trustworthy

(10) According to the passage, describe the grammatical term for 'yield' within the context of the sentence, 'a plentiful yield'.

A   Verb
B   Noun
C   Adjective
D   Metaphor
E   Simile

STOP AND WAIT FOR FURTHER INSTRUCTIONS

Grammar

 YOU HAVE 5 MINUTES TO COMPLETE THE FOLLOWING SECTION.

YOU HAVE 9 QUESTIONS TO COMPLETE WITHIN THE TIME GIVEN.

EXAMPLES

Read the passage below and answer the 9 questions that follow. There are some mistakes in the use of capital letters and punctuation. In some questions there may be no errors.

> The dogs were running in the garden. As the postman opened the gate, the dogs started biting the postman's leg.

Example 1

Look at the following options taken from the above passage. Select the option that contains a punctuation or grammar error, if any.

A	B	C	D	E
The dogs	were	in the	garden	No errors

The correct answer is E. This has already been marked in Example 1 in the Grammar section of your answer sheet.

Practice Question 1

Look at the following options taken from the above passage. Select the option that contains a punctuation or grammar error, if any.

A	B	C	D	E
As the postman	the dogs	biting	the postmans	No errors

The correct answer is D. Please mark the answer D in Practice Question 1 in the Grammar section of your answer sheet.

STOP AND WAIT FOR FURTHER INSTRUCTIONS

Read the passage below and answer the 9 questions that follow. There are some mistakes in the use of capital letters and punctuation. In some questions there may be no errors.

Emily and Laura were sisters. Laura was the elder of the two sisters. They were heading out to drop of some clothes at the local jumble sale. Laura carried a large bag of clothes to the village hall jumble sale. she could not see in front of herself and tripped on the uneven pavement. She nearly got a bad accident. Luckily Emily caught her as she fell. After dropping off the bag of clothes, they had a quick browse at what was on offer.

"This jacket of mine is wore out," remarked Emily. "I'll see if I can get a new one here."

Whilst perusing the clothes, Laura realised she hurted her leg when she nearly fell over earlier. They decided to head home after emily realised there were no suitable jackets to buy. "Lets run home together," said Emily, but after a while Laura said, "I cannot run no further."

Look at the following sentences from the above passage and select the answer from below that has a grammatical or punctuation error, if any.

(1) Laura was the elder of the two sisters.

A	B	C	D	E
Laura	was	elder	sisters	No errors

(2) she could not see in front of herself and tripped on the uneven pavement.

A	B	C	D	E
in front	could not	she	pavement.	No errors

(3) She nearly got a bad accident.

A	B	C	D	E
She	nearly	got	a bad	No errors

(4) "This jacket of mine is wore out," remarked Emily.

A	B	C	D	E
"This	jacket of	out," remarked	is wore out,"	No errors

CONTINUE WORKING

(5) "I'll see if I can get a new one here."

A	B	C	D	E
"I'll	see if	I can get	a new one here."	No errors

(6) Whilst perusing the clothes, Laura realised she hurted her leg when she nearly fell over earlier.

A	B	C	D	E
Whilst perusing	the clothes,	she hurted her leg	when she nearly	No errors

(7) They decided to head home after emily realised there were no suitable jackets to buy.

A	B	C	D	E
They decided to	head home after	emily realised	jackets to buy	No errors

(8) "Lets run home together," said Emily, but after a while Laura said, "I cannot run no further."

A	B	C	D	E
"Lets run	home together,"	said Emily,	but after	No errors

(9) "Lets run home together," said Emily, but after a while Laura said, "I cannot run no further."

A	B	C	D	E
said Emily,	while Laura said,	"I cannot run	no further	No errors

STOP AND WAIT FOR FURTHER INSTRUCTIONS ⬣

Numeracy

INSTRUCTIONS

 YOU HAVE 19 MINUTES TO COMPLETE THE FOLLOWING SECTION.

YOU HAVE 39 QUESTIONS TO COMPLETE WITHIN THE TIME GIVEN.

EXAMPLES

Example 1

Calculate 53 – 42

A   12   **B**   1   **C**   4   **D**   5   **E**   11

The correct answer is E. This has already been marked in Example 1 in the Numeracy section of your answer sheet.

Practice Question 1

Calculate 95 – 75

A   21   **B**   20   **C**   19   **D**   18   **E**   13

The correct answer is B. Please mark this in Practice Question 1 in the Numeracy section of your answer sheet.

STOP AND WAIT FOR FURTHER INSTRUCTIONS

(1) What is the number if 21 is three times more than half of this number?

| **A** | 36 | **B** | 48 | **C** | 126 | **D** | 7 | **E** | 14 |

(2) Select the appropriate number or numbers to complete the sequence in place of the ? in the sequence below.

31, 32, 34, ?, 41

| **A** | 35 | **B** | 36 | **C** | 37 | **D** | 38 | **E** | 39 |

(3) Select the appropriate numbers to complete the subtraction in place of the ? in the incomplete calculation below.

Your choice of answers is written as the missing numbers should appear in the question from left to right.

```
  ? 9 ? 4
-   7 8 ?
---------
  4 ? 3 3
```

| **A** | 4, 1, 1, 1 | **B** | 4, 1, 2, 1 | **C** | 3, 9, 8, 7 |
| **D** | 3, 1, 1, 1 | **E** | 4, 1, 2, 2 | | |

(4) My journey by car across London in the rush hour averages 8 mph. The distance of the journey is 1.6 miles. How long does the journey take?

| **A** | 4 minutes | **B** | 5 minutes | **C** | 16 minutes |
| **D** | 15 minutes | **E** | 12 minutes | | |

(5) Susan works in a café and gets a staff discount of 20% on all food and drink that she purchases there. She has lunch in the café every weekday. She spends £24 each week in the café on her lunch. What is the value of the discount on her food purchased in the café each week?

| **A** | £8 | **B** | £4 | **C** | £5 | **D** | £6 | **E** | £4.80 |

(6) Mohammed is 4 years older than Emily's brother, William. Emily and William are twins. If Emily is 7, how old is Mohammed?

| **A** | 3 | **B** | 11 | **C** | 9 | **D** | 12 | **E** | 4 |

CONTINUE WORKING

7 Arrange the following in order of size, from smallest to largest.

101 mm, 10.11 cm, $\frac{1}{10}$ m, 10 km, 11 cm

A $\frac{1}{10}$ m, 101 mm, 10.11 cm, 11 cm, 10 km

B   101 mm, $\frac{1}{10}$ m, 10.11 cm, 11 cm, 10 km

C $\frac{1}{10}$ m, 10.11 cm, 101 mm, 11 cm, 10 km

D $\frac{1}{10}$ m, 101 mm, 11 cm, 10.11 cm, 10 km

E $\frac{1}{10}$ m, 10km, 101 mm, 10.11 cm, 11 cm

8 Select the only equation that is incorrect.

A $453 - 2 = 452 - 0$
B $5{,}868 - 1{,}869 = 3{,}999$
C $901 = 1001 - 10 \times 10$
D $65 = 3 \times 21 + 2$
E $86 = 50 + 2 \times 18$

9 Calculate 26^2.

A   767   **B**   520   **C**   176   **D**   576   **E**   676

10 Identify the number that the vertical arrow is pointing to on the number line.

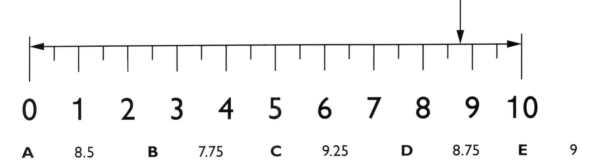

A   8.5   **B**   7.75   **C**   9.25   **D**   8.75   **E**   9

11 Calculate 3 hours and 55 minutes on from 9:25 a.m.

A   12:20 p.m.   **B**   1:20 p.m.   **C**   1 p.m.
D   10:25 a.m.   **E**   11:25 a.m.

CONTINUE WORKING →

(12) Calculate $\frac{1}{3} \div 3$

A $\frac{3}{9}$ B 2   C $\frac{1}{9}$ D $\frac{1}{8}$ E $\frac{4}{6}$

(13) Which number is half way between 23 and 7?

A 15   B 16   C 25   D 15.5   E 14.5

(14) A map has a scale of 1 : 500,000. If two churches are 5 mm apart on the map, how far apart are they in real life?

A 10,000 m   B 6,500 m   C 125 km
D 100 km   E 2,500 m

(15) How many grams are there in 0.52 kg?

A 250   B 52   C 5,200
D 520   E 7

(16) Calculate 1.1% of 70.

A 0.77   B 0.66   C 0.55   D 0.5   E 0.4

(17) Select the number to go in place of the question mark.

$? \times 15 = 75$

A 5   B 4   C 3   D 6   E 7

CONTINUE WORKING ⇨

18 Look at the chart below and answer the question that follows.

The chart shows the favourite hobby of each child in a class.

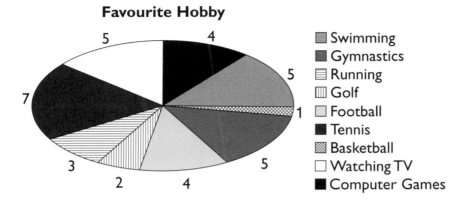

Favourite Hobby

Swimming
Gymnastics
Running
Golf
Football
Tennis
Basketball
Watching TV
Computer Games

Which is the least favourite hobby of the children in the class?

A	Tennis	**B**	Gymnastics	**C**	Watching TV
D	Basketball	**E**	Swimming		

Look at the chart below and answer the questions that follow.

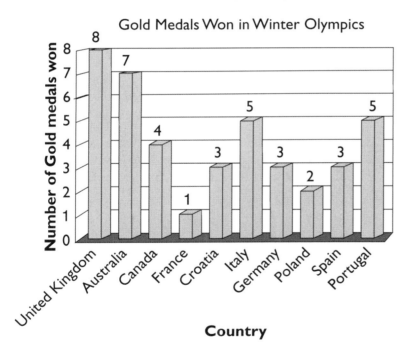

19 What is the mode number of gold medals won?

A	3	**B**	4	**C**	5	**D**	6	**E**	7

CONTINUE WORKING

20 Which country won the second most gold medals?

A	United Kingdom	**B**	Australia	**C**	Portugal
D	Spain	**E**	Germany		

21 What is the median number of medals won?

A 3.5   **B** 3   **C** 4   **D** 5   **E** 6

22 What is the mean number of gold medals won?

A 4   **B** 4.5   **C** 3.1   **D** 4.1   **E** 10

Look at the Venn diagram below, which shows the number of children that like certain types of cars, then answer the questions that follow.

Children

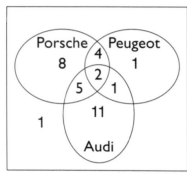

23 How many children like both Audi and Peugeot cars?

A 1   **B** 3   **C** 2   **D** 5   **E** 24

24 Out of all of the children asked, how many do not like Peugeots?

A 24   **B** 13   **C** 25   **D** 16   **E** 12

25 How many children like Porsche cars, but do not like Audi cars?

A 12   **B** 17   **C** 23   **D** 8   **E** 24

CONTINUE WORKING ⇨

(26) How many children like all of Porsche, Audi and Peugeot cars?

    A   3   **B**   32   **C**   7   **D**   2   **E**   6

(27) How many children like Audi and Peugeot cars, but not Porsche cars?

    A   1   **B**   3   **C**   2   **D**   5   **E**   12

(28) Complete the following magic square by choosing the five numbers to go in the place of a, b, c, d and e in the correct order.

Each row, column and diagonal adds up to the same number.

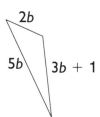

a	b	c
d	e	5
7	1	7

A   3, 9, 3, 5, 3
B   2, 9, 3, 5, 5
C   3, 9, 2, 5, 5
D   3, 9, 3, 3, 5
E   3, 9, 3, 5, 5

(29) A mystery number, p is divided by 10. The result is subtracted from 99. The answer is 89.

Solve the mystery to find the value of p.

    A   10   **B**   100   **C**   109   **D**   1   **E**   0

(30) Mike has five times as many marbles as Julia. Julia has the same number of marbles as Mark. There are 91 marbles in total. How many marbles does Mike have?

    A   39   **B**   13   **C**   26   **D**   65   **E**   60

(31) Look at the triangle below, which shows the lengths of each side in cm.

$2b$

$5b$ $3b + 1$

The perimeter = 101 cm. Calculate the value of b.

    A   20   **B**   8   **C**   10   **D**   15   **E**   21

CONTINUE WOKING

(32) Calculate 17 ÷ 0.15

(Include three digits after the decimal point in your answer.)

| A | 113.333 | B | 112.344 | C | 111.785 |
| D | 113.345 | E | 113.453 | | |

(33) A gymnastics club has 43 people inside. There are 14 adults. There are 35 men and children.

Use the information above to calculate the number of men, women and children.

A   Men 6, women 8, children 29
B   Men 6, women 6, children 31
C   Men 6, women 8, children 27
D   Men 5, women 9, children 29
E   Men 8, women 5, children 29

(34) How many days are there between the following two dates (including the two dates given).

25th April to 14th June

| A | 50 | B | 416 | C | 51 | D | 415 | E | 49 |

(35) The 16.29 coach takes three hours and 45 minutes to arrive at its destination. What time does the coach arrive at its destination?

| A | 20.04 | B | 19.29 | C | 19.14 | D | 21.11 | E | 20.14 |

(36) Look at the quadrilateral below and calculate the size of angle *a*.

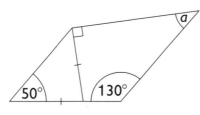

| A | 65° | B | 30° | C | 55° | D | 80° | E | 40° |

CONTINUE WORKING ⇨

37 Look at the quadrilateral below and calculate the size of angle e (not drawn to scale).

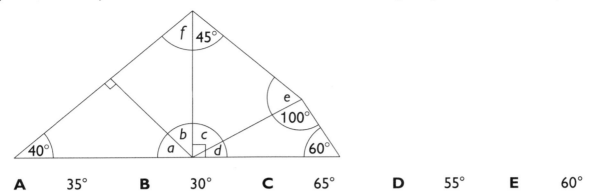

| **A** | 35° | **B** | 30° | **C** | 65° | **D** | 55° | **E** | 60° |

38 Look at the following table showing the rate of exchange between the three currencies. Calculate the number that should go in the place of the ?

GB Pounds	Euros	US Dollars
150	165	225
600	660	900
?	1210	1650

| **A** | 1,150 | **B** | 1,500 | **C** | 1,010 |
| **D** | 1,100 | **E** | 1,350 | | |

39 I am trying to work out the dimensions of a rectangle. The length is 12 times the width. The perimeter is 104 cm. Calculate the length and width of the rectangle.

A   length 48 cm, width 4 cm
B   length 28 cm, width 24 cm
C   length 20 cm, width 32 cm
D   length 12 cm, width 1 cm
E   length 36 cm, width 3 cm

STOP AND WAIT FOR FURTHER INSTRUCTIONS ⊗

Synonyms

INSTRUCTIONS

 YOU HAVE 5 MINUTES TO COMPLETE THE FOLLOWING SECTION.

YOU HAVE 20 QUESTIONS TO COMPLETE WITHIN THE TIME GIVEN.

EXAMPLES

Select the word that is most similar in meaning to the following word:

cold

A	B	C	D	E
collect	fence	foggy	windy	chilly

The correct answer is E. This has already been marked in Example 1 in the Synonyms section of your answer sheet.

Practice Question 1

Select the word that is most similar in meaning to the following word:

start

A	B	C	D	E
cramped	begin	free	without	change

The correct answer is B. Please mark this in Practice Question 1 in the Synonyms section of your answer sheet.

STOP AND WAIT FOR FURTHER INSTRUCTIONS

In each question, identify the word in the table that is most similar in meaning to the given word.

1 assure

A	B	C	D	E
strike	verbose	prohibited	detract	guarantee

2 gracious

A	B	C	D	E
hamlet	pardon	frustration	courteous	stasis

3 frantic

A	B	C	D	E
frenzied	kingdom	arctic	fleeting	confident

4 flourish

A	B	C	D	E
glory	perpetuity	illusion	thrive	alliance

5 fringe

A	B	C	D	E
border	patrol	carousel	amenable	arctic

6 agility

A	B	C	D	E
contend	impertinent	swathe	pious	nimbleness

CONTINUE WORKING ▶

7 uncontrollable

A	B	C	D	E
belief	encounter	unruly	pioneer	rant

8 synthetic

A	B	C	D	E
artificial	fearful	drab	convalescence	drawback

9 royal

A	B	C	D	E
imperial	cartographer	vow	fool	penetrate

10 disguise

A	B	C	D	E
extend	liberal	inconspicuous	masquerade	behaviour

11 flexible

A	B	C	D	E
elude	prosperous	undeniable	supple	deliberate

12 twist

A	B	C	D	E
wring	role	terminus	reposition	assortment

13 impartial

A	B	C	D	E
acclimatise	neutral	guile	celebrated	idler

CONTINUE WORKING ▶

14 overhear

A	B	C	D	E
eavesdrop	correct	understandable	desert	haul

15 understand

A	B	C	D	E
leading	pace	comprehend	gratuity	firm

16 attire

A	B	C	D	E
clothing	disorder	apt	psychiatrist	handicap

17 contest

A	B	C	D	E
erratic	oppose	wail	novice	picture

18 enemy

A	B	C	D	E
coast	pompous	enquire	bustling	foe

19 dishonest

A	B	C	D	E
deceitful	unsanitary	persist	arrogant	yield

20 solve

A	B	C	D	E
flaw	phoney	admission	unravel	persist

STOP AND WAIT FOR FURTHER INSTRUCTIONS

Non-Verbal Reasoning

 YOU HAVE 8 MINUTES TO COMPLETE THE FOLLOWING SECTION.

YOU HAVE 9 QUESTIONS TO COMPLETE WITHIN THE TIME GIVEN.

EXAMPLES

COMPLETE THE SEQUENCE Example 1

Select the picture from below that will complete the sequence in place of the ?

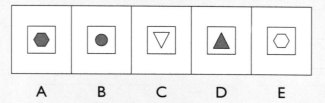

The correct answer is C. This has already been marked in Example 1 in the Non-Verbal Reasoning section of your answer sheet.

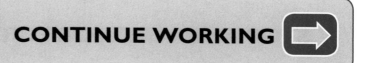

CONTINUE WORKING

COMPLETE THE SEQUENCE Practice Question 1

Select the picture from below that will complete the sequence in place of the ?

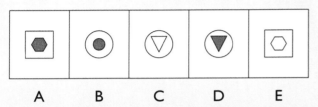

    A   B   C   D   E

The correct answer is D. Please mark this in Practice Question 1 in the Non-Verbal Reasoning section of your answer sheet.

ROTATION Example 2

Select one of the images below that is a rotation of the image on the left.

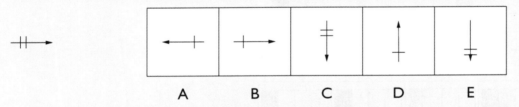

        A   B   C   D   E

The correct answer is C. This has already been marked in Example 2 in the Non-Verbal Reasoning section of your answer sheet.

ROTATION Practice Question 2

Select one of the images below that is a rotation of the image on the left.

 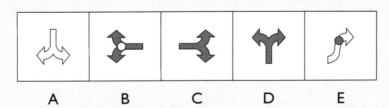

        A   B   C   D   E

The correct answer is B. Please mark this in Practice Question 2 in the Non-Verbal Reasoning section of your answer sheet.

STOP AND WAIT FOR FURTHER INSTRUCTIONS ⊗

Select the pictures which will complete the following sequence:

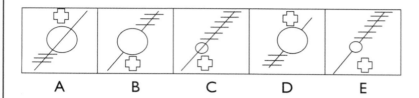

① Select the picture you think should go in place of Q1 here.

② Select the picture you think should go in place of Q2 here.

③ Which pattern completes the sequence in place of the blank grid below?

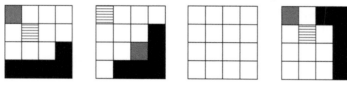

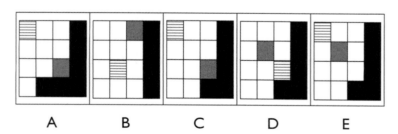

④ Which pattern completes the sequence in place of the blank grid below?

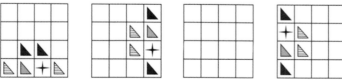

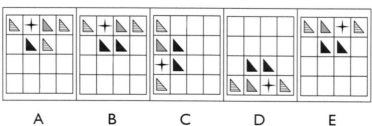

CONTINUE WORKING ▶

(5) Which shape or pattern completes the larger square?

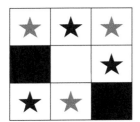

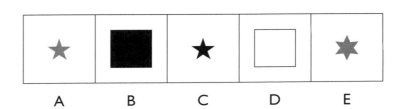

A   B   C   D   E

(6) Which shape or pattern completes the larger square?

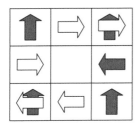

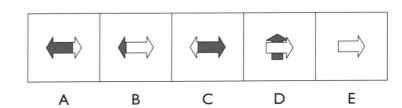

A   B   C   D   E

(7) Which shape or pattern completes the larger square?

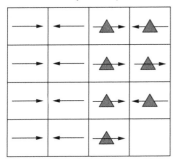

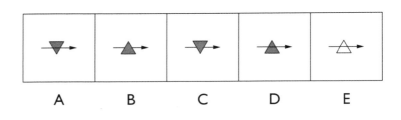

A   B   C   D   E

(8) Select one of the images below that is a rotation of the image on the left.

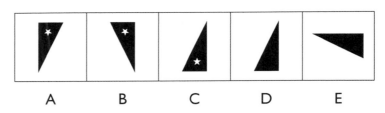

A   B   C   D   E

(9) Select one of the images below that is a rotation of the image on the left.

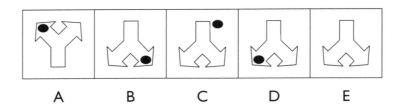

A   B   C   D   E

END OF PAPER

Test C Paper 2

Instructions

1. Ensure you have pencils and an eraser with you.
2. Make sure you are able to see a clock or watch.
3. Write your name on the answer sheet.
4. Do not open the question booklet until you are told to do so by the audio instructions.
5. Listen carefully to the audio instructions given.
6. Mark your answers on the answer sheet only.
7. All workings must be completed on a separate piece of paper.
8. You should not use a calculator, dictionary or thesaurus at any point in this paper.
9. Move through the papers as quickly as possible and with care.
10. Follow the instructions at the foot of each page.
11. You should mark your answers with a horizontal strike, as shown on the answer sheet.
12. If you want to change your answer, ensure that you rub out your first answer and that your second answer is clearly more visible.
13. You can go back and review any questions that are within the section you are working on only. You must await further instructions before moving onto another section.

Symbols and Phrases used in the Tests

 Instructions
 Time allowed for this section
 Stop and wait for further instructions
 Continue working

Cloze Sentences

  INSTRUCTIONS

 YOU HAVE 7 MINUTES TO COMPLETE THE FOLLOWING SECTION.

YOU HAVE 17 QUESTIONS TO COMPLETE WITHIN THE TIME GIVEN.

EXAMPLES

Example 1

Complete the sentence in the most sensible way by selecting the appropriate word from each set of brackets.

The (dog, big, gate) sat on the (mat, open, great).

A   big, open
B   dog, great
C   gate, mat
D   dog, mat
E   dog, open

The correct answer is D. This has already been marked in Example 1 of the Cloze Sentences section of your answer sheet.

Practice Question 1

Complete the sentence in the most sensible way by selecting the appropriate word from each set of brackets.

My name is (Helen, high, sand) and I am (ten, dig, land) years old.

A   Helen, dig
B   high, land
C   sand, land
D   Helen, land
E   Helen, ten

The correct answer is E. Please mark the answer E in Practice Question 1 in the Cloze Sentences section of your answer sheet.

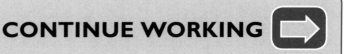
CONTINUE WORKING

Example 2

One word in the following sentence has had three letters removed from it. Keeping the letters in the same order, identify the three-letter word that is made from these missing letters.

The pupil could not pay attion.

The correct answer is 'ten'. This is shown in Example 2 in the Cloze Sentences section of your answer sheet.

Practice Question 2

One word in the following sentence has had three letters removed from it. Keeping the letters in the same order, identify the three-letter word that is made from these missing letters.

She treasu her mother's bracelet.

The correct answer is 'red'. Please write this in Practice Question 2 in the Cloze Sentences section of your answer sheet.

STOP AND WAIT FOR FURTHER INSTRUCTIONS

Complete the most sensible sentence by selecting the appropriate combination of words from within the brackets. Use one word from each set of brackets.

1. The (plumber, dentist, butcher) took time to reassure me before starting work on my (garden, teeth, hair).

   A   plumber, teeth
   B   butcher, hair
   C   butcher, garden
   D   dentist, teeth
   E   dentist, garden

2. (Despite, Hence, During) the shortfall in numbers, a good (time, weather, seasonal) was had by all (art, rent, guests).

   A   Hence, time, rent
   B   During, time, art
   C   Despite, time, guests
   D   Despite, weather, guests
   E   During, time, rent

CONTINUE WORKING

3 They were hoping the (sympathetic, weather, yesterday) would be better than it had been (recently, tomorrow, treasured).

A   yesterday, treasured
B   weather, recently
C   yesterday, tomorrow
D   sympathetic, recently
E   weather, treasured

4 The (support, troubles, health) of the (airport, dream, nation) was behind the athletes.

A   troubles, nation
B   troubles, airport
C   support, nation
D   health, dream
E   troubles, dream

5 The (depth, puppy, temperature) of (sympathy, pool, horses) was very much appreciated by the mourners.

A   depth, pool
B   temperature, pool
C   puppy, horses
D   depth, sympathy
E   depth, horses

6 The (internet, tortoise, ambulance) rushed to the (scene, clouds, music).

A   internet, music
B   tortoise, scene
C   ambulance, scene
D   internet, clouds
E   ambulance, clouds

7 (Where, When, Who) would arrive first was anybody's (dress, guess, blessed).

A   Where, blessed
B   Who, dress
C   When, dress
D   Who, guess
E   Where, guess

CONTINUE WORKING ➡

(8) The (underneath, ultimate, outcome) of the court case was due (imminently, window, grass).

A	underneath, imminently
B	ultimate, grass
C	outcome, imminently
D	underneath, grass
E	ultimate, window

(9) The (monkey, bungalow, empathy) perched on her shoulder and (rug, hastened, smiled) for the (chair, camera, sun).

A	empathy, smiled, camera
B	bungalow, hastened, sun
C	empathy, rug, chair
D	monkey, smiled, camera
E	monkey, rug, sun

(10) How the (direction, completeness, magician) managed to do that, I will (endeavour, never, have) know!

A	direction, have
B	completeness, have
C	magician, never
D	magician, have
E	completeness, endeavour

One word in the following sentence has had three letters removed from it. Keeping the letters in the same order, identify the three-letter word that is made from these three missing letters.

(11) The flowers were attracg the butterflies.

(12) The instabiy of the suspension bridge meant closure was the only option.

(13) The pocopier had run out of paper.

(14) They were feeling confit as they set out on their expedition.

(15) They enjoyed dling their feet in the sea on the hot summer's day.

(16) They decided to meet up the foling month.

(17) ry little detail had been considered.

STOP AND WAIT FOR FURTHER INSTRUCTIONS

Problem Solving

 YOU HAVE 12 MINUTES TO COMPLETE THE FOLLOWING SECTION.

YOU HAVE 10 QUESTIONS TO COMPLETE WITHIN THE TIME GIVEN.

EXAMPLES

A £2.60	B £3.40	C £2.40	D 25	E £1.35
F £3.40	G 14	H 31	I 28	J 34

Example 1

Calculate the following:

If I buy five apples at 20p each, and four bananas at 35p each, how much change will I receive if I pay with a £5 note.

The correct answer is A. This has already been marked in Example 1 in the Problem Solving section of your answer sheet.

Practice Question 1

Calculate the following:

There are 17 people on a bus when it arrives at a bus stop. Eleven people get on the bus, and three get off. How many people are then left on the bus?

The correct answer is D. Please mark this in Practice Question 1 in the Problem Solving section of your answer sheet.

STOP AND WAIT FOR FURTHER INSTRUCTIONS

| **A** 53 | **B** 12 | **C** £527 | **D** £52 | **E** £41.40 |
| **F** 5 | **G** 9 | **H** 10 | **I** 27 | **J** £35.00 |

Read the passage below, then select an answer to each question from the 10 different possible answers in the table above. You may use an answer for more than one question.

Sarah is a pupil at Woodbridge Middle School. There are four girls to every five boys in her class. There are 15 boys in Sarah's class.

Sarah's brother Sam attends the same school and Sam is 4 now. In two years' time, Sarah will be twice as old as her brother Sam.

The number of children that attend the school has grown over the last few years, as a new development of houses was recently built in the area. There are now around 150 pupils in the school. There are 76 children in years 4, 5 and 6 combined.

Every year the school raises money for a charity. Sarah is collecting money for the charity from her class, and has completed a sponsored walk. All of the pupils in her class donated £1, except two children who gave £2 each, and six children who donated £5 each. Sarah did not donate any money.

As the number of pupils attending Woodbridge Middle School is growing, the school governors have decided to improve the school by building new classrooms, and refreshing the current classrooms. Sarah's classroom requires a new floor. The dimensions of the floor are 8 m by 4 m. Most of the improvements to the school are being completed at the weekends when the school is always closed.

Part of the money to improve the school is being raised from an increase in the cost of school lunches for the children. These increased by 20p on Wednesday 1st March to £1.80.

Also, in order to raise money, the class organised a raffle for the school fete. A number of prizes were donated, and there was also a special cash prize of £100. The £100 was allocated from the money raised from selling raffle tickets. Ticket sales were as follows:

123 books of tickets were sold at £5 per book.

60 individual tickets were also sold at 20p per ticket.

1 How many children are there in Sarah's class?

2 How old is Sarah now?

3 If there are 23 children in Year 5, how many children are there in years 4 and 6 combined?

CONTINUE WORKING

(4) How much did Sarah raise for charity from her class?

(5) If the tiles used to cover the floor in Sarah's classroom are 50 cm by 50 cm, and come in boxes of 15, how many boxes of tiles are required to cover the entire floor?

(6) Sarah has added up all of the girls' shoe sizes, and they total 60. What is the mean shoe size of the girls in Sarah's class?

(7) How much does Sarah spend on her lunch in March, if she is not absent for any of the school days?

(8) The school buys plastic cups in tubes of 200. If 10 cups cost 3.5p, how much do 50 tubes of plastic cups cost?

(9) In school assembly one morning, there are 174 people in the room. Of these people:

- boys and teachers make up 99 people

- girls and teachers make up 87 people.

How many teachers are in the room?

(10) How much was raised by the raffle after all the prizes were claimed?

STOP AND WAIT FOR FURTHER INSTRUCTIONS

Antonyms

 YOU HAVE 10 MINUTES TO COMPLETE THE FOLLOWING SECTION.

YOU HAVE 25 QUESTIONS TO COMPLETE WITHIN THE TIME GIVEN.

EXAMPLES

Example 1

Which word is least similar to the following word:

light

A	B	C	D	E
dark	water	feather	bright	hill

The correct answer is A. This has already been marked in Example 1 in the Antonyms section of your answer sheet.

Practice Question 1

Which word is least similar to the following word:

smooth

A	B	C	D	E
allow	beneath	rough	whilst	shade

The correct answer is C. Please mark the answer C in Practice Question 1 in the Antonyms section of your answer sheet.

STOP AND WAIT FOR FURTHER INSTRUCTIONS

Which word is least similar to the following word:

(1) fresh

A	B	C	D	E
board	stale	silence	increase	indeed

(2) stationary

A	B	C	D	E
unsurprised	phone	perilous	mobile	paper

(3) steep

A	B	C	D	E
home	reject	bold	separate	gradual

(4) straight

A	B	C	D	E
crooked	merry	bright	gentle	success

(5) superior

A	B	C	D	E
contaminated	silence	dull	inferior	shrink

(6) tame

A	B	C	D	E
prohibit	sweet	wild	preserve	modest

CONTINUE WORKING

7 tiny

A	B	C	D	E
fade	incompetent	decrease	enormous	advance

8 unite

A	B	C	D	E
separate	imprudent	selfish	absurd	follower

9 vacant

A	B	C	D	E
height	relaxed	unfriendly	occupied	disperse

10 clear

A	B	C	D	E
reduce	valour	sober	fondness	vague

11 better

A	B	C	D	E
fade	generous	genuine	reaction	worse

12 combine

A	B	C	D	E
contract	separate	fertile	loose	crooked

13 encourage

A	B	C	D	E
courage	impolite	guilty	discourage	mild

CONTINUE WORKING ➡

14 import

A	B	C	D	E
strict	cavity	indirect	legal	export

15 brighten

A	B	C	D	E
fade	trick	delight	stale	disobedient

16 boundless

A	B	C	D	E
limited	gradual	admit	increase	occupied

17 decrease

A	B	C	D	E
admiration	separate	increase	abundant	genuine

18 admit

A	B	C	D	E
fail	mobile	legal	immigration	deny

19 action

A	B	C	D	E
displeasure	constant	inaction	loose	often

CONTINUE WORKING ▶

20 enigmatic

A	B	C	D	E
clear	graceful	innocent	minute	ally

21 changeable

A	B	C	D	E
allay	separate	constant	imprudent	smart

22 pleasure

A	B	C	D	E
fail	encouraged	simple	disperse	displeasure

23 order

A	B	C	D	E
hinder	bright	stale	singular	disorder

24 amateur

A	B	C	D	E
modern	professional	usual	disloyal	cramped

25 domestic

A	B	C	D	E
foreign	mobile	introvert	mild	shrink

STOP AND WAIT FOR FURTHER INSTRUCTIONS

Non-Verbal Reasoning

INSTRUCTIONS

 YOU HAVE 8 MINUTES TO COMPLETE THE FOLLOWING SECTION.

YOU HAVE 15 QUESTIONS TO COMPLETE WITHIN THE TIME GIVEN.

EXAMPLES

CODES Example 1

Look at the codes for the following patterns and identify the missing code for the pattern on the far right.

					A	BE
					B	AD
					C	BC
					D	BD
AD	AE	BD	CE		E	CD

The correct answer is E. This has already been marked in Example 1 in the Non-Verbal Reasoning section of your answer sheet.

CODES Practice Question 1

Look at the codes for the following patterns and identify the missing code for the pattern on the far right.

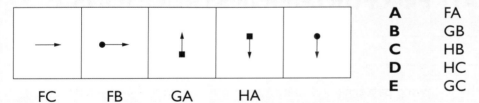

				A	FA
				B	GB
				C	HB
				D	HC
FC	FB	GA	HA	E	GC

The correct answer is C. Please mark this in Practice Question 1 in the Non-Verbal Reasoning section of your answer sheet.

CONTINUE WORKING

COMPLETE THE SQUARE Example 2

Which shape or pattern completes the square?

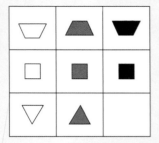 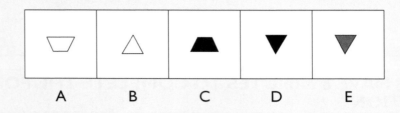

The correct answer is D. This has already been marked in Example 2 in the Non-Verbal Reasoning section of your answer sheet.

COMPLETE THE SQUARE Practice Question 2

Which shape or pattern completes the square?

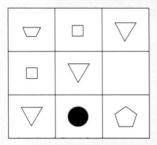 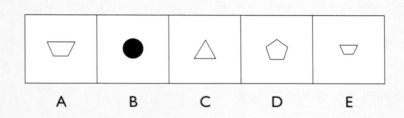

The correct answer is B. Please mark this in Practice Question 2 in the Non-Verbal Reasoning section of your answer sheet.

STOP AND WAIT FOR FURTHER INSTRUCTIONS

(1) Look at the codes for the following patterns and identify the missing code for the pattern on the far right.

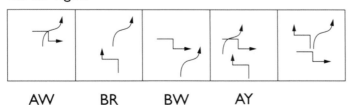

A	BY
B	AR
C	AY
D	BW
E	BR

AW   BR   BW   AY

CONTINUE WORKING

2) Look at the codes for the following patterns and identify the missing code for the pattern on the far right.

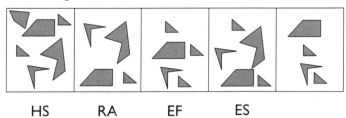

HS	RA	EF	ES

A   EF
B   RF
C   RA
D   RS
E   EA

3) Look at the codes for the following patterns and identify the missing code for the pattern on the far right.

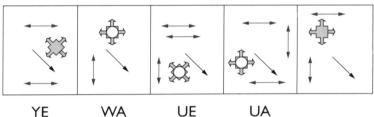

LD	HD	YS	HA

A   LH
B   HD
C   LB
D   YS
E   YA

4) Look at the codes for the following patterns and identify the missing code for the pattern on the far right.

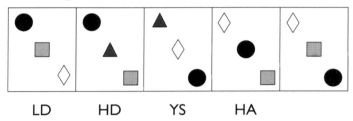

YE	WA	UE	UA

A   WA
B   YA
C   WE
D   UA
E   YE

5) Look at the two shapes on the left immediately below.
Find the connection between them and apply it to the third shape.

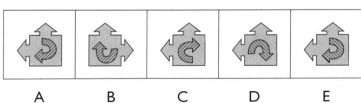

A	B	C	D	E

CONTINUE WORKING

(6) Look at the two shapes on the left immediately below.
Find the connection between them and apply it to the third shape.

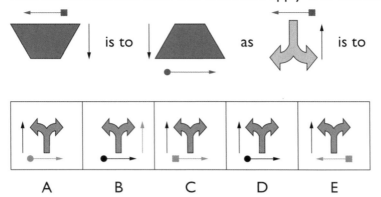

A	B	C	D	E

(7) Look at the two shapes on the left immediately below.
Find the connection between them and apply it to the third shape.

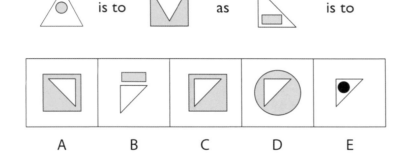

A	B	C	D	E

(8) Look at the two shapes on the left immediately below.
Find the connection between them and apply it to the third shape.

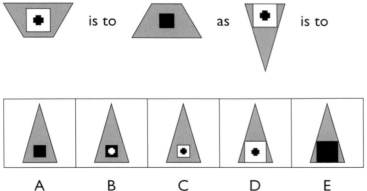

A	B	C	D	E

CONTINUE WORKING

9 Select the correct picture from the bottom row in order to finish the incomplete sequence on the top row.

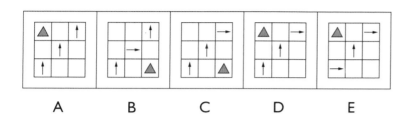

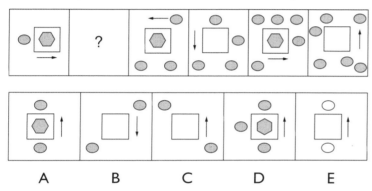

A B C D E

10 Select the picture from below that will complete the sequence in place of the?

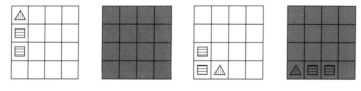

A B C D E

11 Which pattern completes the sequence in place of the blank grid below?

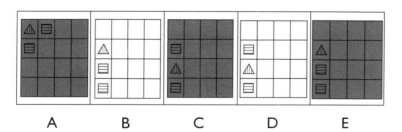

A B C D E

CONTINUE WORKING ➡

(12) Which pattern completes the sequence in place of the blank grid below?

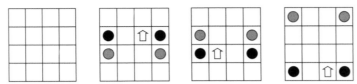

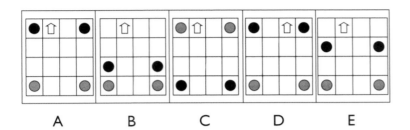

A   B   C   D   E

(13) Which shape or pattern completes the larger square?

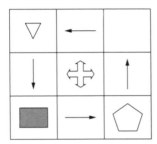

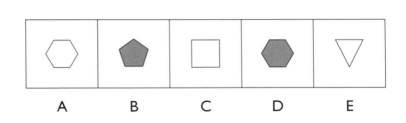

A   B   C   D   E

(14) Which shape or pattern completes the larger square?

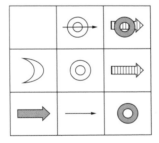

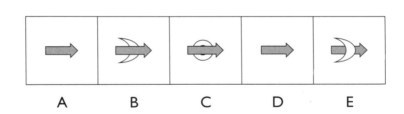

A   B   C   D   E

(15) Which shape or pattern completes the larger square?

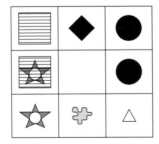

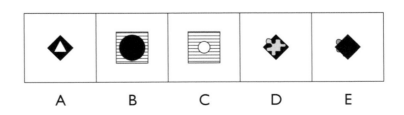

A   B   C   D   E

STOP AND WAIT FOR FURTHER INSTRUCTIONS ✖

Shuffled Sentences

 INSTRUCTIONS

 YOU HAVE 8 MINUTES TO COMPLETE THE FOLLOWING SECTION.

YOU HAVE 15 QUESTIONS TO COMPLETE WITHIN THE TIME GIVEN.

EXAMPLES

Example 1

The following sentence is shuffled and also contains one unnecessary word. Rearrange the sentence correctly, in order to identify the unnecessary word.

dog the ran fetch the to stick gluing.

A	B	C	D	E
gluing	dog	ran	the	stick

The correct answer is A. This has already been marked in Example 1 in the Shuffled Sentences section of your answer sheet.

Practice Question 1

The following sentence is shuffled and also contains one unnecessary word. Rearrange the sentence correctly, in order to identify the unnecessary word.

pushed Emma stood up and closed the table under the chairs.

A	B	C	D	E
chairs	stood	under	closed	Emma

The correct answer is D. Please mark this in Practice Question 1 in the Shuffled Sentences section of your answer sheet.

STOP AND WAIT FOR FURTHER INSTRUCTIONS

The following sentence is shuffled and also contains one unnecessary word. Rearrange the sentence correctly, in order to identify the unnecessary word.

(1) a strewn streets was night's the neighbourhood's across storm of last result debris as an.

A	B	C	D	E
an	night's	result	debris	strewn

(2) airport delays caused the bad weather to severe whether flights at the.

A	B	C	D	E
whether	bad	flights	airport	severe

(3) this big difference is likely to make those a.

A	B	C	D	E
difference	likely	big	those	this

(4) the leaf in the tree decided to she through book bookshop whilst.

A	B	C	D	E
tree	through	whilst	decided	book

(5) although it was now the parents of the responsibility.

A	B	C	D	E
it	now	parents	although	responsibility

(6) checked all the scores there were confirm to their accuracy.

A	B	C	D	E
were	there	accuracy	confirm	scores

CONTINUE WORKING ⇨

7 seen she by what was she had scene astounded just.

A	B	C	D	E
she	astounded	scene	what	was

8 the ideal central location was mirrored for them.

A	B	C	D	E
them	central	ideal	mirrored	the

9 was the hallway positioned in the hanging basket.

A	B	C	D	E
hanging	was	in	hallway	the

10 to recover the several attempts were made cargo sunk.

A	B	C	D	E
attempts	sunk	recover	cargo	made

11 the journey taken car hours by three took.

A	B	C	D	E
car	journey	took	taken	hours

12 the ball dress kicked code stipulated for annual formal the attire charity.

A	B	C	D	E
kicked	ball	stipulated	charity	formal

13 provided the storage chest bedroom drawers waist extra of in the.

A	B	C	D	E
waist	drawers	extra	storage	of

CONTINUE WORKING

(14) must use the theatre prohibited of was cameras in.

A	B	C	D	E
prohibited	use	theatre	must	cameras

(15) was in accept a payment return for cash offered discount in.

A	B	C	D	E
discount	accept	cash	in	for

END OF PAPER

Test D Paper 1

Instructions

1. Ensure you have pencils and an eraser with you.

2. Make sure you are able to see a clock or watch.

3. Write your name on the answer sheet.

4. Do not open the question booklet until you are told to do so by the audio instructions.

5. Listen carefully to the audio instructions given.

6. Mark your answers on the answer sheet only.

7. All workings must be completed on a separate piece of paper.

8. You should not use a calculator, dictionary or thesaurus at any point in this paper.

9. Move through the papers as quickly as possible and with care.

10. Follow the instructions at the foot of each page.

11. You should mark your answers with a horizontal strike, as shown on the answer sheet.

12. If you want to change your answer, ensure that you rub out your first answer and that your second answer is clearly more visible.

13. You can go back and review any questions that are within the section you are working on only. You must await further instructions before moving onto another section.

Symbols and Phrases used in the Tests

 Instructions  Time allowed for this section Stop and wait for further instructions  Continue working

Comprehension

 YOU HAVE 10 MINUTES TO COMPLETE THE FOLLOWING SECTION.

YOU HAVE 10 QUESTIONS TO COMPLETE WITHIN THE TIME GIVEN.

EXAMPLES

Comprehension Example

Some people choose to start their Christmas shopping early in October. It has been reported that some people even buy their Christmas presents in the sales in August. In recent years, people have the option of purchasing their Christmas presents online.

Example 1

According to the passage, what is the earliest that people start their Christmas shopping?

A   In the preceding summer
B   In the preceding October
C   In the preceding November
D   Christmas Eve
E   In early December

The correct answer is A. This has already been marked in Example 1 in the Comprehension section of your answer sheet.

Practice Question 1

In recent years, what has caused a change in how people shop?

A   There are more shops
B   Shops are more crowded
C   You can easily organise your journey to the shops
D   New products are available
E   There has been a rise in use of the Internet

The correct answer is E. Please mark this in Practice Question 1 in the Comprehension section of your answer sheet.

STOP AND WAIT FOR FURTHER INSTRUCTIONS

Read the following passage, then answer the questions below.

A Perspective on the Changing World of Communication

Communication has developed over the millennia at a phenomenal rate. It continues to develop and, as a result, the world has become unrecognisable for many older people.

Communication is made up of verbal communication (spoken), non-verbal communication (body language) and the written word.

Face-to-face communication is complex and subtle messages are often conveyed through body language and eye movements. Many people now study these signs to learn how to read the signals that the person is unintentionally giving away, rather than just listening to the words which are being spoken. People wish to master these signals to enhance their business skills and to assist their career path. People also study this for interpersonal relations outside of the business environment.

Interpreting signals from body language seems quite the opposite of communication via emails and texts, which do not have the benefit of facial expressions and body language to help convey the right message. The tone of emails can easily be misconstrued. When writing an email, it is very important to choose words carefully and read the whole email to check how the email will be interpreted by the recipient. To reintroduce some sort of human emotion, many people also include icons or 'emoticons' in their texts and emails, such as a 'smiley face'. Instantly, the recipient is given the message that this email or text has happy and informal content.

In the context of the business world, emails have drastically reduced the time it takes to communicate to large numbers of people within an organisation, or between organisations. Teams of people can easily be brought together for a meeting via video calls, often saving a huge amount of time and money on travel. The decisions and actions which are a result of these meetings, the 'Minutes', can be communicated easily, cheaply and quickly. In the business environment, icons are inappropriate and should be avoided.

Many people now receive so many emails that it is unmanageable to read and respond to the vast majority of them. As people receive so many emails, many remain unread and are simply deleted. As people become aware that the detail in emails is often skimmed over, people's communication styles have changed. It is advised that lengthy emails should be avoided, unless it is absolutely necessary to write more.

People are now almost always contactable by phone and it is hard to think that just over thirty years ago the first commercially available mobile phones were the size of a household brick and limited to phone calls only. Since then, the size of mobile phones has reduced and the tasks which can be performed on them have broadened. People are able to run their social lives as well as their business lives via 'apps', which is the shortened word for 'applications'. It could be said that people now communicate less by phone, as many would prefer to text or communicate via social media.

CONTINUE WORKING

How different the world is now. A person born in the early to mid-20th century has seen so many fundamental changes in the world, that it has become unrecognisable. Many elderly people find that communicating using today's technology is out of this world and incomprehensible; whereas technology is the norm to most young people. There are now many initiatives which seek to assist elderly people to understand how to use the Internet. Subsequently, elderly people can then learn how to use social media to keep them in touch with their families. In addition, they can complete tasks such as online shopping, online banking and memory games.

(1) What signals are important in face-to-face communication?

    A   The spoken word only
    B   The written word
    C   Body language and eye movements
    D   Signals written on the wall
    E   Emails only

(2) Why do people study body language for business purposes?

    A   To be able to understand what people are saying
    B   To make their emails more coherent
    C   To understand foreign languages
    D   To enhance interpersonal relationships
    E   To further their career and to bring them success

(3) What is the meaning of 'misconstrued'?

    A   Miscalculated
    B   Misdial
    C   Misunderstood
    D   Mislead
    E   Misbehaved

(4) According to the passage, what are the benefits of email communication regarding meetings?

    A   The meetings have to be attended by many people
    B   The meetings are shorter
    C   The details from the meetings are instantly recorded
    D   The details from the meetings can be easily sent to a significant amount of people
    E   The details from the meetings can be typed up easily

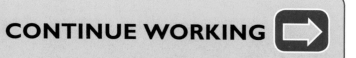

CONTINUE WORKING

(5) According to the passage, which phrase below best describes how mobile phones have developed?

A   Mobiles phones are now often used in business meetings
B   The size of mobile phones has reduced and their capabilities have increased
C   Mobile phones have not dramatically changed or developed
D   Mobile phones have replaced verbal communication
E   The size of mobile phones has reduced and the use of them is limited

(6) According to the passage, what often happens to emails which are received?

A   A large number of emails are unread or deleted
B   Almost all emails are read and responded to
C   Very few emails are deleted
D   Many emails are forwarded to large amounts of people
E   Many emails are lengthy and are always read

(7) In the context of the passage, what type of word is 'household'?

A   Noun
B   Adjective
C   Verb
D   Pronoun
E   Adverb

(8) What is the meaning of 'commonplace'?

A   A place that everyone knows
B   An item that is low in quality
C   An item that people use in their everyday life
D   An item that is rarely used
E   An item that is easy to understand

(9) In the context of the passage, which of the words below is the opposite of 'incomprehensible'?

A   User-friendly
B   Unfriendly
C   Unintelligible
D   Compatible
E   Sensible

(10) Which phrase best describes the final paragraph in the passage?

A   Elderly people understand the changes in technology
B   Most elderly people use social media daily
C   Elderly people are being taught how to communicate via social media
D   Many young people are teaching elderly people how to use the Internet
E   Elderly people are being taught the dangers of social media

STOP AND WAIT FOR FURTHER INSTRUCTIONS

Numeracy

INSTRUCTIONS

 YOU HAVE 17 MINUTES TO COMPLETE THE FOLLOWING SECTION.

YOU HAVE 28 QUESTIONS TO COMPLETE WITHIN THE TIME GIVEN.

EXAMPLES

Example 1

Calculate 53 – 42

A 12 **B** 1 **C** 4 **D** 5 **E** 11

The correct answer is E. This has already been marked in Example 1 in the Numeracy section of your answer sheet.

Practice Question 1

Calculate 95 – 75

A 21 **B** 20 **C** 19 **D** 18 **E** 13

The correct answer is B. Please mark this in Practice Question 1 in the Numeracy section of your answer sheet.

STOP AND WAIT FOR FURTHER INSTRUCTIONS

(1) $36{,}048 \div 12$

    A 3,040 **B** 304 **C** 4,003 **D** 3,004 **E** 34

(2) $12^2 - 11^2$

    A 144 **B** 23 **C** 133 **D** 10 **E** 165

③ $\frac{1}{3}$ of 294

A   102   **B**   97   **C**   96   **D**   9   **E**   98

④ What is the size of each interior angle in a pentagon?

A   72°   **B**   62°   **C**   105°   **D**   108°   **E**   150°

⑤ Find a, if $b = 2a - 4$ and $b = 4$

A   0   **B**   8   **C**   4   **D**   2   **E**   1

⑥ If $b = 8$, find a using the following equation:

$8a - b = 0$

A   8   **B**   2   **C**   0   **D**   1   **E**   4

⑦ Find the missing number marked by?

$5 \times 3 + ? = 20$

A   1   **B**   5   **C**   4   **D**   17   **E**   10

⑧ Find the missing number marked by?

$8 \times ? - 8 = 72$

A   1   **B**   10   **C**   5   **D**   8   **E**   17

⑨ Find the missing number marked by?

$? + 5 \times 3 = 30$

A   1   **B**   5   **C**   2   **D**   4   **E**   15

⑩ If wrapping paper costs £1.50 per metre, how many rolls can I buy for £10? Each roll is 3 m long.

A   6   **B**   3   **C**   2   **D**   15   **E**   30

CONTINUE WORKING

(11) I have just rolled a 4 on a die. The die is a fair die with 6 sides.

What is the probability that the next time I roll the die, I will roll a 4?

A	1 in 4	**B**	1 in 3	**C**	1 in 16
D	1 in 36	**E**	1 in 6		

(12) Calculate the answer to the following:

(25 ÷ 5) + 22 − 11 = ?

A	16	**B**	38	**C**	27	**D**	6	**E**	15

(13) I am sharing out a large pizza between guests at a party. There are 20 guests. A quarter of the guests have said they would not like any pizza. The pizza is cut into equal sized slices. A third of the guests who wanted pizza did not have time to eat their pizza. How many pieces of pizza are remaining?

A	4	**B**	5	**C**	7	**D**	6	**E**	10

(14) What is the first number in this sequence marked by ?

? , 29, 24, 20, 17, 15

A	34	**B**	33	**C**	35	**D**	28	**E**	31

(15) What is half of 52?

A	25	**B**	24	**C**	26	**D**	31	**E**	35

(16) I have 56 sweets that I am sharing out equally amongst my 6 friends and myself. How many 7s can I take away from 56?

A	7	**B**	8	**C**	6	**D**	5	**E**	10

(17) The news headlines are repeated on a television channel precisely every 15 minutes. How many times are the headlines shown on the television channel each day?

A	144	**B**	95	**C**	40	**D**	96	**E**	48

CONTINUE WORKING ⏵

(18) What is the next number in the sequence?

0.1, 0.2, 0.4, 0.8, ?

A   1.6   B   0.16   C   0.10   D   0.12   E   0.18

(19) Which amount is largest?

A   one-quarter of 124
B   one-fifth of 160
C   one-tenth of 315
D   half of 62
E   one-third of 94

(20) There are five people in a room. After a while, three of the people leave the room and a further seven people enter the room. How many people are now in the room?

A   5   B   3   C   4   D   7   E   9

The following three questions relate to the chart shown below:

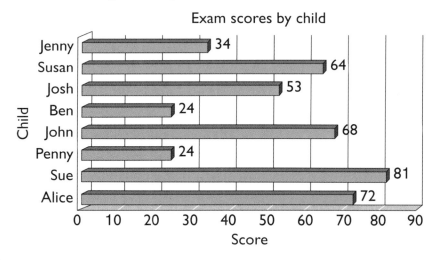

Exam scores by child

(21) What is the range?

A   24   B   52   C   35   D   57   E   81

(22) What is the mean exam score?

A   52.5   B   55   C   50   D   24   E   81

CONTINUE WORKING

(23) What is the median exam score?

A 56   **B** 81   **C** 58.5   **D** 54   **E** 35

The following five questions relate to the chart shown below:

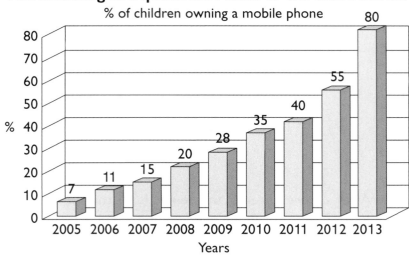

% of children owning a mobile phone

(24) What percentage of children owned a mobile phone in the year 2011?

A 25   **B** 35   **C** 40   **D** 20   **E** 15

(25) Between which two years did the percentage of children owning a mobile phone increase by five times exactly?

A 2006–2012   **B** 2005–2009   **C** 2011–2013
D 2008–2013   **E** 2000–2007

(26) Between which two consecutive years did the percentage of children owning a mobile phone increase the most?

A 2004–2005   **B** 2001–2002   **C** 2007–2008
D 2009–2010   **E** 2012–2013

(27) Calculate the mean percentage of children owning a mobile phone over the period shown.

A 31   **B** 34   **C** 32 and $\frac{1}{3}$
D 23 and $\frac{1}{4}$ **E** 25 and $\frac{1}{5}$

(28) If the mean percentage of children owning a mobile phone increases to 38 over the period to 2014 (from 2005), what is the percentage of children who owned a mobile phone in 2014?

A 65   **B** 60   **C** 75   **D** 89   **E** 100

STOP AND WAIT FOR FURTHER INSTRUCTIONS

Synonyms

 YOU HAVE 9 MINUTES TO COMPLETE THE FOLLOWING SECTION.

YOU HAVE 20 QUESTIONS TO COMPLETE WITHIN THE TIME GIVEN.

EXAMPLES

Example 1

Select the word that is most similar in meaning to the following word:

cold

A	B	C	D	E
collect	fence	foggy	windy	chilly

The correct answer is E. This has already been marked in Example 1 in the Synonyms section of your answer sheet.

Practice Question 1

Select the word that is most similar in meaning to the following word:

start

A	B	C	D	E
cramped	begin	free	without	change

The correct answer is B. Please mark this in Practice Question 1 in the Synonyms section of your answer sheet.

STOP AND WAIT FOR FURTHER INSTRUCTIONS

In each row, identify the word in the table that is most similar in meaning to the word above the table.

(1) daily

A	B	C	D	E
irregularly	routinely	seldom	momentous	calmly

(2) falsify

A	B	C	D	E
verify	rectify	easily	distort	validate

(3) vigour

A	B	C	D	E
vitality	lethargy	apathy	balanced	caged

(4) blossom

A	B	C	D	E
notion	infer	fritter	crazed	unfold

(5) recollect

A	B	C	D	E
dial	remember	perverse	despise	recourse

(6) organisation

A	B	C	D	E
intermittent	company	alcove	consensus	arrested

CONTINUE WORKING ⇨

7 vintage

A	B	C	D	E
misshapen	advantageous	classic	inopportune	contemporary

8 disclosure

A	B	C	D	E
hone	tumbler	pious	shifting	admission

9 energetic

A	B	C	D	E
multitude	spirited	passive	insolent	motionless

10 thanks

A	B	C	D	E
restless	denial	emptiness	gratitude	anomaly

11 hasten

A	B	C	D	E
hurry	improvement	dawdle	periodic	beautiful

12 quantity

A	B	C	D	E
thoughtless	conviction	delightful	averse	amount

13 ravage

A	B	C	D	E
entail	devour	sustenance	revelry	triumph

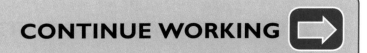

CONTINUE WORKING

14 sophisticated

A	B	C	D	E
squalid	derogatory	deplorable	reluctant	civilised

15 genial

A	B	C	D	E
genius	detract	unhappy	detestable	happy

16 radiate

A	B	C	D	E
bard	emanate	aligned	deduce	foolish

17 courteous

A	B	C	D	E
enshroud	affray	polite	pliable	suggest

18 serene

A	B	C	D	E
rounded	glaring	pomp	tranquil	honour

19 diminish

A	B	C	D	E
nifty	lessen	increase	equality	lesson

20 course

A	B	C	D	E
glut	attentive	series	sterile	affectionate

STOP AND WAIT FOR FURTHER INSTRUCTIONS ⊗

Non-Verbal Reasoning

INSTRUCTIONS

 YOU HAVE 9 MINUTES TO COMPLETE THE FOLLOWING SECTION.

YOU HAVE 15 QUESTIONS TO COMPLETE WITHIN THE TIME GIVEN.

EXAMPLES

REFLECTION Example 1

Select an image from the row below that shows how the following shape or pattern will appear when reflected.

The correct answer is E. This has already been marked in Example 1 in the Non-Verbal Reasoning section of your answer sheet.

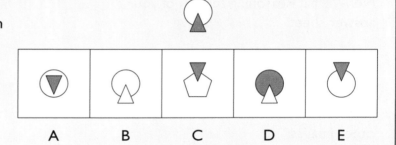

REFLECTION Practice Question 1

Select an image from the row below that shows how the following shape or pattern will appear when reflected.

The correct answer is C. Please mark this in Practice Question 1 in the Non-Verbal Reasoning section of your answer sheet.

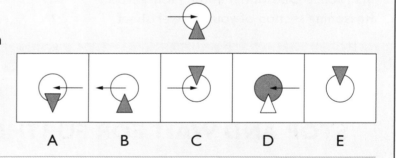

ROTATION Example 2

Select an image from the row below that is a rotation of the following image.

The correct answer is C. This has already been marked in Example 2 in the Non-Verbal Reasoning section of your answer sheet.

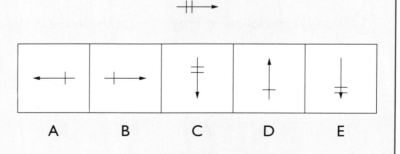

CONTINUE WORKING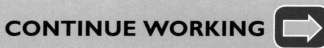

ROTATION Practice Question 2

Select an image from the row below that is a rotation of the following image.

The correct answer is B. Please mark this in Practice Question 2 in the Non-Verbal Reasoning section of your answer sheet.

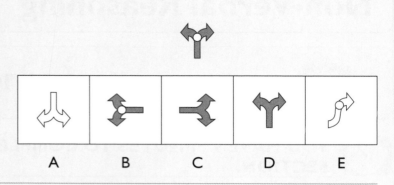

A   B   C   D   E

LEAST SIMILAR Example 3

Select the image that is least similar to the other images.

The correct answer is B. This has already been marked in Example 3 in the Non-Verbal Reasoning section of your answer sheet.

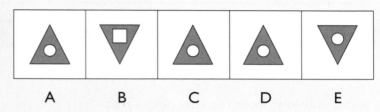

A   B   C   D   E

LEAST SIMILAR Practice Question 3

Select the image that is least similar to the other images.

The correct answer is E. Please mark this in Practice Question 3 in the Non-Verbal Reasoning section of your answer sheet.

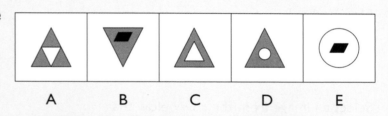

A   B   C   D   E

STOP AND WAIT FOR FURTHER INSTRUCTIONS

(1) Look at the following image. Select the image in the row below that is a rotation of the image.

 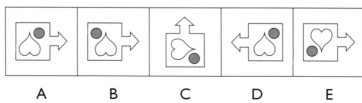

A   B   C   D   E

CONTINUE WORKING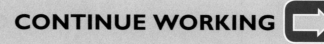

(2) Look at the following image. Select the image in the row below that is a rotation of the image.

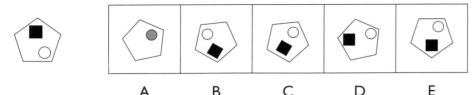

A   B   C   D   E

(3) Select the image that is least similar to the other images in the row.

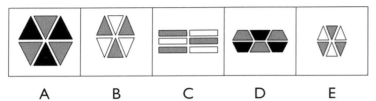

A   B   C   D   E

(4) Select the image that is least similar to the other images in the row.

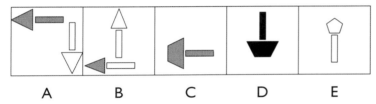

A   B   C   D   E

(5) Select the image that is least similar to the other images in the row.

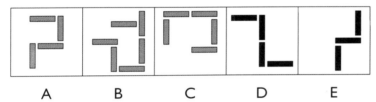

A   B   C   D   E

(6) Select the image that is least similar to the other images in the row.

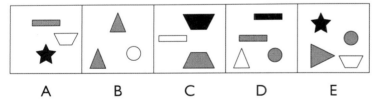

A   B   C   D   E

(7) Select the image that is least similar to the other images in the row.

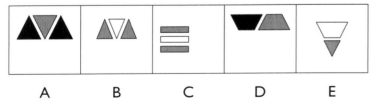

A   B   C   D   E

CONTINUE WORKING ▢⟶

(8) Select the image that is least similar to the other images in the row.

A   B   C   D   E

(9) Select the image that is least similar to the other images in the row.

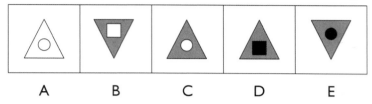

A   B   C   D   E

(10) Select the image that is least similar to the other images in the row.

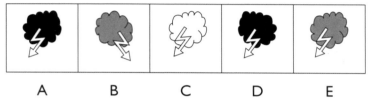

A   B   C   D   E

(11) Select the image that is least similar to the other images in the row.

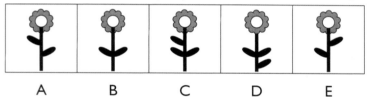

A   B   C   D   E

(12) Select the image that is least similar to the other images the row.

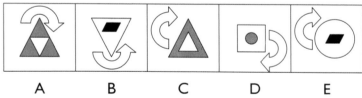

A   B   C   D   E

(13) Select an image from the row below that shows how the following image will appear when reflected in the dashed line.

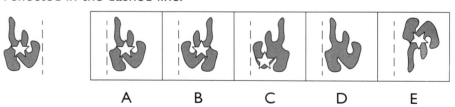

A   B   C   D   E

CONTINUE WORKING

14 Select an image from the row below that shows how the following image will appear when reflected in the dashed line.

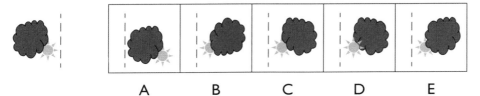

A   B   C   D   E

15 Select an image from the row below that shows how the following image will appear when reflected in the dashed line.

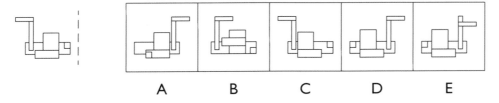

A   B   C   D   E

END OF PAPER

Test D Paper 2

Instructions

1. Ensure you have pencils and an eraser with you.
2. Make sure you are able to see a clock or watch.
3. Write your name on the answer sheet.
4. Do not open the question booklet until you are told to do so by the audio instructions.
5. Listen carefully to the audio instructions given.
6. Mark your answers on the answer sheet only.
7. All workings must be completed on a separate piece of paper.
8. You should not use a calculator, dictionary or thesaurus at any point in this paper.
9. Move through the papers as quickly as possible and with care.
10. Follow the instructions at the foot of each page.
11. You should mark your answers with a horizontal strike, as shown on the answer sheet.
12. If you want to change your answer, ensure that you rub out your first answer and that your second answer is clearly more visible.
13. You can go back and review any questions that are within the section you are working on only. You must await further instructions before moving onto another section.

Symbols and Phrases used in the Tests

 Instructions

 Time allowed for this section

 Stop and wait for further instructions

 Continue working

Cloze Sentences

  INSTRUCTIONS

 YOU HAVE 7 MINUTES TO COMPLETE THE FOLLOWING SECTION.

YOU HAVE 17 QUESTIONS TO COMPLETE WITHIN THE TIME GIVEN.

EXAMPLES

A	B	C	D	E	F	G	H	I	J
dog	small	tiny	huge	minute	free	big	enormous	gigantic	penguin

Example 1

Complete the sentence in the most sensible way by selecting an appropriate word from the table above.

The _____ sat by the fire.

The correct answer is A. This has already been marked in Example 1 in the Cloze Sentences section of your answer sheet.

Practice Question 1

Complete the sentence in the most sensible way by selecting an appropriate word from the table above.

The _____ laid an egg.

The correct answer is J. Please mark the answer J in Practice Question 1 in the Cloze Sentences section of your answer sheet.

Example 2

One word in the following sentence has had three letters removed from it. Keeping the letters in the same order, identify the three-letter word that is made from the missing letters.

The pupil could not pay attion.

The correct answer is 'ten'. This has been marked in Example 2 in the Cloze Sentences section of your answer sheet.

CONTINUE WORKING

Practice Question 2

One word in the following sentence has had three letters removed from it. Keeping the letters in the same order, identify the three-letter word that is made from the missing letters.

She treasu her mother's bracelet.

The correct answer is 'red'. Please mark this in Practice Question 2 in the Cloze Sentences section of your answer sheet.

STOP AND WAIT FOR FURTHER INSTRUCTIONS

Complete the most sensible sentence by selecting an appropriate word from the table below.

A	fantastical	B	dehydrated	C	laborious	D	fractured	E	subterranean
F	extracted	G	ruling	H	standard	I	ample	J	adventure

(1) The blood was _____ from the ancient specimen.

(2) The judge's _____ was final.

(3) The _____ cave was dark and cold.

(4) The parking signs gave the residents _____ warning that the road would close at midnight.

(5) The work was painstaking and _____.

(6) The animal's limb was _____ in several places.

(7) The journey came to an end and the _____ was over.

CONTINUE WORKING

(8) The film was a _____ story, set in space.

(9) The athlete's dedication to her training had set a high _____.

(10) After a day of walking in the mountains, the boy felt _____.

One word in the following sentence has had three letters removed from it. Keeping the letters in the same order, identify the three-letter word that is made from the three missing letters.

(11) The hairdresser tmed the girl's hair.

(12) The landse was rugged.

(13) The project failed for one rea.

(14) The boy hed in the glorious sunshine.

(15) The girl's clothes were sped when she splashed in the mud.

(16) Does this car have a sp tyre?

(17) The se of the book had broken and all the pages had fallen out.

STOP AND WAIT FOR FURTHER INSTRUCTIONS ⬡✕

Problem Solving

INSTRUCTIONS

 YOU HAVE 12 MINUTES TO COMPLETE THE FOLLOWING SECTION.

YOU HAVE 10 QUESTIONS TO COMPLETE WITHIN THE TIME GIVEN.

EXAMPLES

A £2.60	B £3.40	C £2.40	D 25	E £1.35
F £3.40	G 14	H 31	I 28	J 34

Example 1

Calculate the following:

If I buy five apples at 20p each, and four bananas at 35p each, how much change will I receive if I pay with a £5 note.

The correct answer is A. This has already been marked in Example 1 in the Problem Solving section of your answer sheet.

Practice Question 1

Calculate the following:

There are 17 people on a bus when it arrives at a bus stop. Eleven people get on the bus, and three get off. How many people are then left on the bus?

The correct answer is D. Please mark this in Practice Question 1 in the Problem Solving section of your answer sheet.

STOP AND WAIT FOR FURTHER INSTRUCTIONS

Several questions will follow for you to answer.

A 35	B £104	C 8	D 10	E 95
F 7	G 85	H £84	I £94	J 4

Select an answer to each question from the 10 different possible answers in the table above.
You may use an answer for more than one question.

(1) Edward is planning a birthday party at the local zoo. He invites eight boys and four girls. If $\frac{3}{4}$ of the children invited attend the party, and there are two girls at the party, how many boys are at the party (including Edward himself)?

(2) How many children are at the party in total?

(3) At the entrance to the zoo, the following entry prices are displayed:
   Adults £12 each
   Children £8 each
   For groups of 11 or more, £7 (per adult or child)
If two adults also go to the zoo to supervise the children, what is the total entry cost for the party?

(4) Edward receives some gifts and money from his friends and family for his birthday. He receives a £10 note from each of four friends, £20 from one family member, and a £5 note from each of six other people. Finally, he receives a birthday card with four £1 coins taped inside. How much money did Edward receive for his birthday?

(5) At lunchtime, there is a birthday party lunch at the zoo for everyone in the party group. The zoo provides a set party lunch for each of the adults and children. The cost is £8.50 per child and £9.50 per adult. What is the total cost of the party lunch?

(6) Everyone sits down for lunch at 13:05 and the lunch finishes at 14:40. How long did the lunch last in minutes?

(7) Following lunch, the group decide to go on the zoo train that carries visitors around the zoo. The train stops at various places around the zoo. When the entire party boarded the train, there were already 68 people on board. At the next stop, 13 other zoo visitors alight from the train, and a further 18 visitors board the train. How many people are on the train at that point?

CONTINUE WORKING

(8) The next stop for the train is the tiger and lion enclosures, which are very popular. 78 of the passengers alight from the train at this point. Nobody is able to board the train at this stop. How many people are on the train after the 78 people have alighted?

(9) The party get off the train at the final destination which is the aquarium. The time at this point is 15:25. How many minutes were they on board the train if they first boarded the train at 14:50?

(10) The group left the aquarium quite late in the day. The train had stopped running for the day at this point. The group had only 15 minutes to reach the exit of the zoo before it was locked at 5 p.m. If the zoo exit was 1 km from the aquarium, at what speed in km/h did they have to walk in order to reach the exit at closing time, at the latest?

STOP AND WAIT FOR FURTHER INSTRUCTIONS

Antonyms

 YOU HAVE 10 MINUTES TO COMPLETE THE FOLLOWING SECTION.

YOU HAVE 25 QUESTIONS TO COMPLETE WITHIN THE TIME GIVEN.

Examples

Example 1

Select the word that is least similar to the following word:

light

A	B	C	D	E
dark	water	feather	bright	hill

The correct answer is A. This has already been marked in Example 1 in the Antonyms section of your answer sheet.

Practice Question 1

Select the word that is least similar to the following word:

smooth

A	B	C	D	E
allow	beneath	rough	whilst	shade

The correct answer is C. Please mark the answer C in Practice Question 1 in the Antonyms section of your answer sheet.

STOP AND WAIT FOR FURTHER INSTRUCTIONS

In each row, select the word from the table that is least similar to the word above the table.

(1) educated

A	B	C	D	E
familiar	uninformed	mourning	forgiveness	unusual

(2) implausible

A	B	C	D	E
nimble	vulgar	frenetic	logical	impossible

(3) pensioner

A	B	C	D	E
proficient	impressionable	draft	infant	inept

(4) bald

A	B	C	D	E
sulk	restriction	flair	custom	hairy

(5) customer

A	B	C	D	E
modest	tradesman	sense	retreat	direct

(6) neglect

A	B	C	D	E
nourish	congeal	outgoing	urgency	refinement

CONTINUE WORKING

(7) glistening

A	B	C	D	E
dull	friendship	gleaming	timely	tangle

(8) casual

A	B	C	D	E
digress	slovenly	interior	planned	result

(9) occupy

A	B	C	D	E
fickle	vacate	agitated	resort	retrieve

(10) invigorated

A	B	C	D	E
receptacle	jovial	tired	slender	vivid

(11) compress

A	B	C	D	E
superlative	restrain	mirth	determine	expand

(12) debt

A	B	C	D	E
profit	fad	fiscal	verdict	spectre

CONTINUE WORKING

13 glamorous

A	B	C	D	E
immaterial	plain	commode	majestic	attractive

14 auxiliary

A	B	C	D	E
prudent	harrowing	main	apprehend	gaunt

15 uneven

A	B	C	D	E
detested	predictive	merriment	level	revelation

16 truth

A	B	C	D	E
beg	rumour	parameter	unkempt	gumption

17 concentrate

A	B	C	D	E
earnest	profanity	dilute	solitude	tendency

18 subdue

A	B	C	D	E
aggravate	forecast	typical	quell	subtlety

CONTINUE WORKING

19 minute

A	B	C	D	E
estimate	inhibit	timely	colossal	immature

20 demolish

A	B	C	D	E
rotund	destruct	resent	undulation	assemble

21 stable

A	B	C	D	E
equilibrium	imbalanced	jovial	reveal	august

22 love

A	B	C	D	E
fondness	beloved	enamoured	animosity	devotion

23 finale

A	B	C	D	E
elitist	opening	jaunt	conclusion	supreme

24 leader

A	B	C	D	E
tireless	consume	follower	guide	shaded

25 mundane

A	B	C	D	E
recapitulate	severe	drowsy	exciting	innate

STOP AND WAIT FOR FURTHER INSTRUCTIONS ⊗

Non-Verbal Reasoning

INSTRUCTIONS

YOU HAVE 8 MINUTES TO COMPLETE THE FOLLOWING SECTION.

YOU HAVE 15 QUESTIONS TO COMPLETE WITHIN THE TIME GIVEN.

EXAMPLES

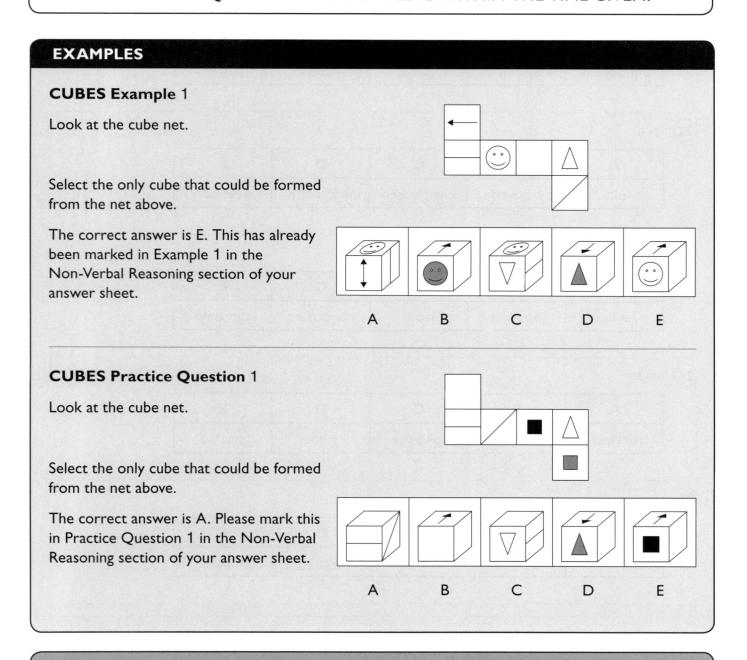

CUBES Example 1

Look at the cube net.

Select the only cube that could be formed from the net above.

The correct answer is E. This has already been marked in Example 1 in the Non-Verbal Reasoning section of your answer sheet.

CUBES Practice Question 1

Look at the cube net.

Select the only cube that could be formed from the net above.

The correct answer is A. Please mark this in Practice Question 1 in the Non-Verbal Reasoning section of your answer sheet.

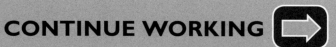

CONTINUE WORKING

REFLECTION Example 2

Select an image from the row below that shows how the following shape or pattern will appear when reflected.

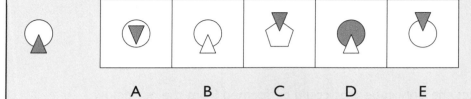

The correct answer is E. This has already been marked in Example 2 in the Non-Verbal Reasoning section of your answer sheet.

REFLECTION Practice Question 2

Select an image from the row below that shows how the following shape or pattern will appear when reflected.

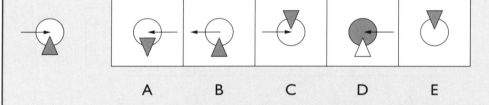

The correct answer is C. Please mark this in Practice Question 2 in the Non-Verbal Reasoning section of your answer sheet.

STOP AND WAIT FOR FURTHER INSTRUCTIONS

① Look at the cube net. Select the only cube that could be formed from the net below.

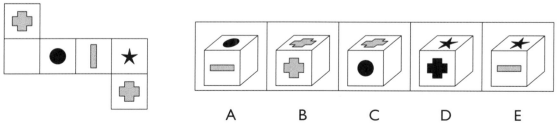

CONTINUE WORKING

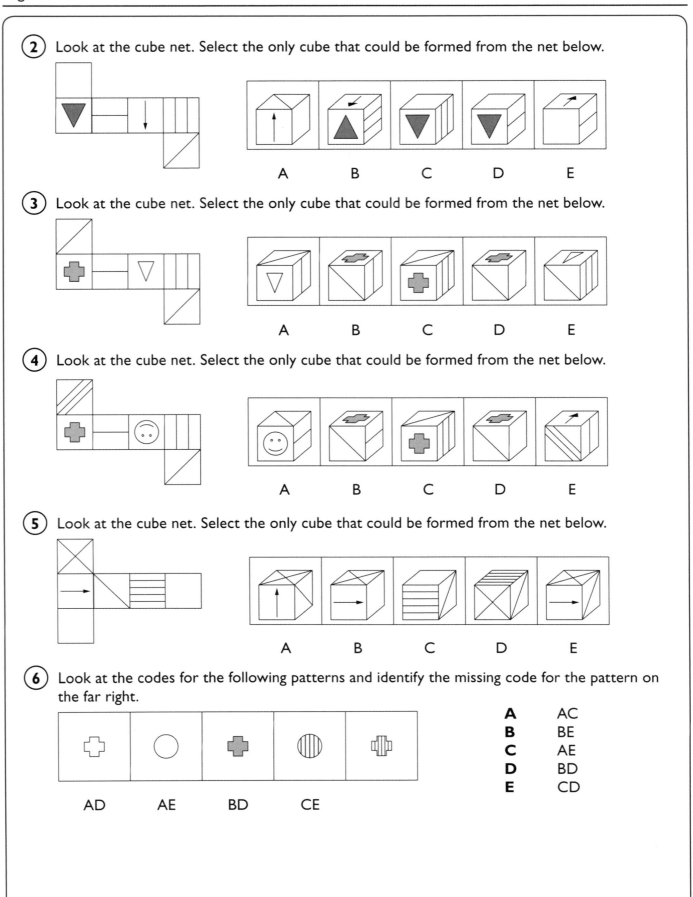

(2) Look at the cube net. Select the only cube that could be formed from the net below.

A   B   C   D   E

(3) Look at the cube net. Select the only cube that could be formed from the net below.

A   B   C   D   E

(4) Look at the cube net. Select the only cube that could be formed from the net below.

A   B   C   D   E

(5) Look at the cube net. Select the only cube that could be formed from the net below.

A   B   C   D   E

(6) Look at the codes for the following patterns and identify the missing code for the pattern on the far right.

AD   AE   BD   CE

A   AC
B   BE
C   AE
D   BD
E   CD

CONTINUE WORKING ➡

(7) Look at the codes for the following patterns and identify the missing code for the pattern on the far right.

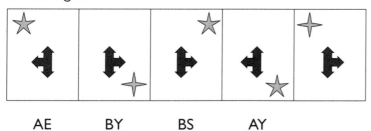

AE   BY   BS   AY

A   BS
B   AS
C   BE
D   AE
E   BY

(8) Look at the codes for the following patterns and identify the missing code for the pattern on the far right.

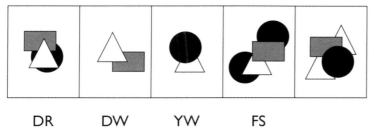

DR   DW   YW   FS

A   YS
B   FS
C   DS
D   DY
E   YR

(9) Look at the codes for the following patterns and identify the missing code for the pattern on the far right.

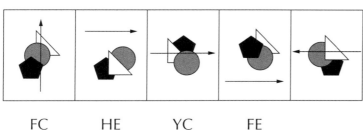

FC   HE   YC   FE

A   HE
B   YC
C   HC
D   FE
E   FY

(10) Look at the codes for the following patterns and identify the missing code for the pattern on the far right.

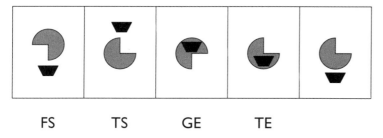

FS   TS   GE   TE

A   TS
B   GE
C   GS
D   FE
E   FS

CONTINUE WORKING ⏩

(11) Look at the codes for the following patterns and identify the missing code for the pattern on the far right.

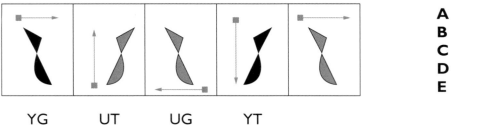

YG   UT   UG   YT

A   YU
B   YG
C   YT
D   UG
E   UT

(12) Select an image from the row below that shows how the following shape or pattern will appear when reflected.

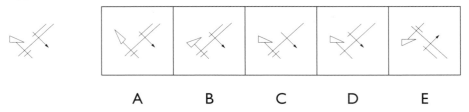

A   B   C   D   E

(13) Select an image from the row below that shows how the following shape or pattern will appear when reflected.

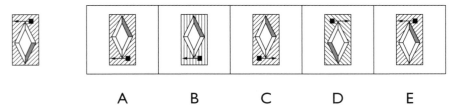

A   B   C   D   E

(14) Select an image from the row below that shows how the following shape or pattern will appear when reflected.

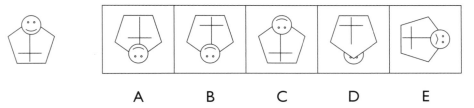

A   B   C   D   E

(15) Select an image from the row below that shows how the following shape or pattern will appear when reflected.

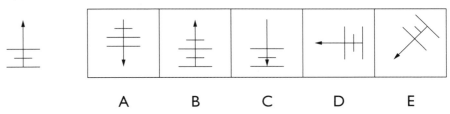

A   B   C   D   E

Shuffled Sentences

INSTRUCTIONS

 YOU HAVE 8 MINUTES TO COMPLETE THE FOLLOWING SECTION.

YOU HAVE 15 QUESTIONS TO COMPLETE WITHIN THE TIME GIVEN.

EXAMPLES

Example 1

The following sentence is shuffled and also contains one unnecessary word.
Rearrange the sentence correctly, in order to identify the unnecessary word.

dog the ran fetch the to stick gluing.

A	B	C	D	E
gluing	dog	ran	the	stick

The correct answer is A. This has already been marked in Example 1 in the Shuffled Sentences section of your answer sheet.

Practice Question 1

The following sentence is shuffled and also contains one unnecessary word.
Rearrange the sentence correctly, in order to identify the unnecessary word.

pushed Emma stood up and closed the table under the chairs.

A	B	C	D	E
chairs	stood	under	closed	Emma

The correct answer is D. Please mark this in Practice Question 1 in the Shuffled Sentences section of your answer sheet.

STOP AND WAIT FOR FURTHER INSTRUCTIONS

Each of the following sentences is shuffled and also contains one unnecessary word. Rearrange the sentence correctly, in order to identify the unnecessary word.

① beautiful sea shelled house overlooking live we but the small a in.

A	B	C	D	E
shelled	a	house	overlooking	the

② chimney misty moonlit the stars in twinkled the sky was and air the.

A	B	C	D	E
and	chimney	misty	was	the

③ unbeatable shop noisy overpriced discounts was advert the stated but the.

A	B	C	D	E
but	was	the	stated	noisy

④ entrance van site candidly the the of the at parked was.

A	B	C	D	E
the	site	candidly	was	van

⑤ hand by mine ancient dug digger was the subterranean

A	B	C	D	E
digger	dug	the	by	hand

⑥ sunrise sight stirred emotions tears the of my the.

A	B	C	D	E
the	tears	of	my	sight

⑦ in test marks tables achieved boy the full achievement times his.

A	B	C	D	E
to	achieved	achievement	went	tables

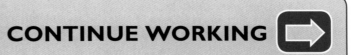

CONTINUE WORKING

8 stabilised enforced steel tunnel the with was.

A	B	C	D	E
the	was	tunnel	enforced	with

9 unemployment many problem countries in is a high there.

A	B	C	D	E
there	countries	in	problem	a

10 shone the dazzling sunlight in the packet diamond.

A	B	C	D	E
diamond	shone	in	the	packet

11 bag landed collected he school son as missing was his noticed he that from his.

A	B	C	D	E
his	was	landed	that	from

12 talking questions the the carefully listen have you elongated answer to people to to.

A	B	C	D	E
talking	to	you	the	elongated

13 rounded bag evidence a in the placed he.

A	B	C	D	E
in	placed	a	rounded	he

14 up for let's view hill go the run a.

A	B	C	D	E
let's	view	a	the	for

CONTINUE WORKING ⇨

15 looked looking plant strange at this look.

A	B	C	D	E
look	at	this	looking	looked

END OF PAPER

Answers to Test C Paper 1

Comprehension

1 C
Verb

2 A
Allotments are very popular

3 E
Allotments require people to spend time and effort.

4 D
Nothing happens

5 B
A busy place

6 A
A large quantity

7 D
Envelop

8 E
Every seven days

9 D
Repel

10 B
Noun

Grammar

1 E
No errors

2 C
she

3 C
got

4 D
is wore out,"

5 E
No errors

6 C
she hurted her leg

7 C
emily realised

8 A
"Lets run

9 D
no further

Numeracy

Q1 E
14, as 7 (a third of 21) is half the number

Q2 C
37, +1 +2 +3 +4 are the differences between consecutive numbers in the sequence

Q3 A
4,1,1,1 as 4 − 1 = 3 in the units column, then in the tens column, the original number must have been 1 which when 1 hundred is borrowed and converted into tens makes the original 1 into 11, and 11 − 8 = 3. The 9 in the hundreds column has now become an 8, so 8 − 7 = 1, and 4 − 0 = 4 in the thousands column.

Q4 E
12 minutes, 8 miles per hour (or 60 minutes) means 1.6 miles will be travelled in 1.6 ÷ 8 × 60 = 12 minutes.

Q5 D
£6, as £24 is the price paid after the discount i.e. 80% of the original price. So 20% must be £24 ÷ 4 = £6.

Q6 B
11, Emily and William are twins, so are the same age (7). Mohammed is 4 years older, 7 + 4 = 11 years old.

Q7 A
$\frac{1}{10}$ m, 101 mm, 10.11 cm, 11 cm, 10 km, as there are 100 cm in 1 m and 1,000 mm in 1 m. Converting all options to cm gives: 10 cm, 10.1 cm, 10.11 cm, 11 cm, 1,000,000 cm

Q8 A
453 − 2 = 452 − 0, as 451 is not the same as 452, and the other answer options are all equal on left and right sides of the equation.

Q9 E
676, as 26 × 20 = 520, and 6 × 26 = 156, 520 + 156 = 676

Q10 D
8.75 midway between 8.5 and 9

Q11 B
1 : 20 p.m. (add 4 hours to get 1 : 25 pm, and then deduct 5 minutes)

Q12 C
$\frac{1}{9}$, as to make the fraction 3 times smaller requires multiplying the denominator by 3.

Q13 A

15, 23 + 7 = 30 and half of 30 is 15

Q14 E

2,500 m, converted to cm in real life the churches are 0.5 × 500,000 = 250,000 cm apart = 2,500 m (by dividing by 100)

Q15 D

520 as there are 1,000 g in 1 kg, so it is necessary to multiply by 1,000.

Q16 A

0.77, 1% of 70 is $\frac{1}{100}$ of 70 = 0.7. So 1.1% of 70 is 1.1 times 0.7, or 0.7 + 0.07 = 0.77

Q17 A

5, as 5 × 15 = 75

Q18 D

basketball, identified by the smallest segment of the chart with the lowest number of children choosing this hobby.

Q19 A

3 as the mode is the most frequently occurring piece of data.

Q20 B

Australia, which has the second highest number of medals after the UK.

Q21 A

3.5, arranging the 10 pieces of data in order of size gives 1,2,3,3,3,4,5,5,7,8 and the median is the middle of this data (in this case the middle of 2 numbers as there is an even number of pieces of data). Halfway between the 5th and 6th pieces of data is 3.5.

Q22 D

4.1 as the sum of all of the data is 41. The mean is calculated by dividing this by the number of pieces of data, which gives an answer of 4.1.

Q23 B

3 as this is the overlapping section of the data sets.

Q24 C

25, i.e. 8 + 5 + 11 + 1 = 25 which is the sum of all numbers outside of the Peugeot set.

Q25 A

12, which is 8 + 4, this is represented by the area within the Porsche set but excluding any numbers that may be within the Audi set (so exclude the 5 + 2).

Q26 D

2 because they are represented by the overlapping part of all 3 sets.

Q27 A

1 represented by the overlapping Audi and Peugeot set which is not within the Porsche set (so need to exclude the 2).

Q28 E

3, 9, 3, 5, 5

The sum of the bottom row is 15, so all rows columns and diagonals sum to 15 (as noted in the question). Next calculate c is 3, then e is 5, so d is 5. Then a must be 3, and finally b is 9.

Q29 B

100, $99 - \frac{p}{10} = 89$, so $\frac{p}{10}$ must be 10, and so p must be 100.

Q30 D

65, dividing the marbles up in the ratio 5:1:1 gives both Julia and Mark 91 divided by 7 (5 + 1 + 1) = 13 marbles each. Mike has 91 ÷ 7 × 5 = 65 marbles.

Q31 C

10, as the perimeter is 10b + 1 = 101, so 10b = 100, and b is therefore 10.

Q32 A

113.333 (make question easier by multiplying both numbers by 100 to eliminate the decimal point to give 1,700 divided by 15)

Q33 A

men 6, women 8, children 29

Women = 43 − 35 = 8, and this means of the 14 adults, 6 must be men, which in turn means that 29 of the 35 men and children are actually children.

Q34 C

51 (1 + 5 + 31 + 14 = 51) The 1 must be added in as the dates are inclusive in the question.

Q35 E

20.14 as 16.29 add 3 hours and 45 minutes gives 20.14 (could add on 4 hours then subtract 15 minutes).

Q36 E

40°

The left triangle is isosceles in which 2 of the angles are 50°, and the other angle is 80°

which is at the bottom right of the triangle. Using the fact that all of the interior angles in the quadrilateral (4 sided shape) sum to 360°, the missing angle is calculated as 360° − 130° − 50° − 50° − 90° = 40°

Q37 C

65°

Angle d is 180° − 100° − 60° = 20°.
So angle c is 70°. So angle e must be 180° − 70° − 45° = 65°

Q38 D

1100

Can work out either the Euro to Pounds exchange rate of 660 ÷ 600 = 1.1 or Dollar to Pound exchange rate of 900 ÷ 600 = 1.5 from the data given in the table.
Use either of these to calculate the number of pounds. 1,210 ÷ 1.1 = 1,100 or 1,650 ÷ 1.5 = 1,100

Q39 A

length 48 cm, width 4 cm
Write length (l) in terms of width (w) to establish perimeter in terms of width,
Perimeter = w + 12w + w + 12w = 26w
Perimeter from question is 104 cm
So 26w = 104
w = 4, so l = 48 (12 × 4)
Alternatively the same method could be followed by writing the width in terms of length, but this may be more challenging.

Synonyms

Q1 E guarantee
Q2 D courteous
Q3 A frenzied
Q4 D thrive
Q5 A border
Q6 E nimbleness
Q7 C unruly
Q8 A artificial
Q9 A imperial
Q10 D masquerade
Q11 D supple
Q12 A wring
Q13 B neutral
Q14 A eavesdrop
Q15 C comprehend
Q16 A clothing
Q17 B oppose
Q18 E foe
Q19 A deceitful
Q20 D unravel

Non-Verbal Reasoning

Q1 D

Alternating circle size, increasing count on horizontal lines, background is diagonal line, foreground circle.

Q2 C

Alternating circle size, increasing count on horizontal lines, small circle should be in the background, with diagonal line in the foreground.

Q3 D

Outer line of five black squares are moving around the outside of the overall grid in an anti-clockwise direction, grey squares moving diagonally towards top left, and striped square always follows grey.

Q4 B

Five triangles and the star are moving anti-clockwise around the overall grid. Alternating outer and inner are solid black triangles and striped triangles. Within triangles are star and grey triangle, again alternating position.

Q5 D

The arrows switch between pointing left and right, as well as alternating between being in the background and foreground in relation to the triangle.

Q6 B

Each row has one grey and one white arrow. These are combined in the other square on each row, with the white always in the foreground and grey in the background. Diagonal from bottom left to top right is sum of other 2 in row, with white in the foreground.

Q7 B

Each column has one of each of the three images featured in the overall grid. The black square is the missing square in the middle column.

Q8 B

Others are reflections or do not include all of the image.

Q9 D

A is a reflection of the image on the left. Must ensure that the dot remains in the same relative position to the arrow when the overall image is rotated.

Answers to Test C Paper 2

Cloze Sentences

Q1 D
dentist, teeth
The dentist took time to reassure me before
starting work on my teeth.

Q2 C
Despite, time, guests
Despite the shortfall in numbers, a good time
was had by all guests.

Q3 B
weather, recently
They were hoping the weather would be
better than it had been recently.

Q4 C
support, nation
The support of the nation was behind the
athletes.

Q5 D
depth, sympathy
The depth of sympathy was very much
appreciated by the mourners.

Q6 C
ambulance, scene
The ambulance rushed to the scene.

Q7 D
Who, guess
Who would arrive first was anybody's guess.

Q8 C
outcome, imminently
The outcome of the court case was due
imminently.

Q9 D
monkey, smiled, camera
The monkey perched on her shoulder and
smiled for the camera.

Q10 C
magician, never
How the magician managed to do that,
I will never know!

Q11 tin
The flowers were attracting the butterflies.

Q12 lit
The instability of the suspension bridge
meant closure was the only option.

Q13 hot
The photocopier had run out of paper.

Q14 den
They were feeling confident as they set out
on their expedition.

Q15 pad
They enjoyed paddling their feet in the sea
on the hot summer's day.

Q16 low
They decided to meet up the following
month.

Q17 Eve
Every little detail had been considered.

Problem Solving

Q1 I
27
There are $15 \div 5 \times 4$ girls = 12 girls and 15
boys = 27 children in the class.

Q2 H
10
Sam is 6 in two years' time, so Sarah will
then be 12. Now (two years earlier), Sarah is
10.

Q3 A
53
$76 - 23 = 53$ children.

Q4 D
£52
$27 - 1 = 26$ children (excluding Sarah);
$6 \times £5 + 2 \times £2 + (26 - 8) \times £1 = £52$

Q5 G
9
Floor area = $8 \times 4 = 32$ square metres. 4
tiles (2×2) will fit exactly into each square
metre. So $4 \times 32 = 128$ tiles are
required to cover the floor. $128 \div 15 = 8$
remainder 8, so 9 boxes will be required.

Q6 F
5
60 divided by 12

Q7 E
£41.40
$23 \times 1.80 = £41.40$

Q8 J
£35
Each tube costs $20 \times 3.5 = 70p$, so 50
tubes cost £35

Q9 B
12
Girls = 174 − 99 = 75, so teachers
= 87 − 75 = 12

Q10 C
£527
Money raised = 123 × £5 = £615 from the
books of tickets. Individual tickets raised a
further 60 × 20p = £12. Total is £615 + £12
= £627. £100 special prize is deducted from
the £627 to leave £527.

Antonyms

Q1 **B** stale	Q14 **E** export
Q2 **D** mobile	Q15 **A** fade
Q3 **E** gradual	Q16 **A** limited
Q4 **A** crooked	Q17 **C** increase
Q5 **D** inferior	Q18 **E** deny
Q6 **C** wild	Q19 **C** inaction
Q7 **D** enormous	Q20 **A** clear
Q8 **A** separate	Q21 **C** constant
Q9 **D** occupied	Q22 **E** displeasure
Q10 **E** vague	Q23 **E** disorder
Q11 **E** worse	Q24 **B** professional
Q12 **B** separate	Q25 **A** foreign
Q13 **D** discourage		

Non-Verbal Reasoning

Q1 A
BY
First letter relates to whether arrows cross or not, second letter relates to the appearance of the non curved arrow(s).

Q2 D
RS
First letter relates to number of shapes, second letter relates to the number of triangles.

Q3 E
YA
First letter relates to shape at the bottom, second letter relates to the shape at the top.

Q4 B
YA
First letter relates to number of double ended arrows, second letter relates to orientation of the square shape with the arrows coming from it.

Q5 A
Connection is outer arrow is rotated a quarter turn anti-clockwise. Also inner arrow is rotated clockwise.

Q6 A
Large shape turns upside down, dark arrow switches from the right hand side of the large shape to left hand side. Light arrow changes from the top to the bottom, also changes direction from pointing left to pointing right and changes the arrow base from a square to circle.

Q7 C
Outer shape is inverted (reflected in a horizontal line), inner grey shape transforms into a large grey square.

Q8 A
The outer shape is inverted, the middle square has become black and smaller. The cross disappears.

Q9 D
The triangle alternates from top left to bottom right corners, the horizontal arrow moves up the diagonal from bottom left to top right. The other arrows remain vertical.

Q10 C
The arrows rotate anti-clockwise around the perimeter of the square. The number of circles increases and the inner hexagon appears in alternate squares as the sequence progresses.

Q11 C
The triangle moves through the sequence of three shapes, from back to front as the sequence progresses. The triangle will be in the middle of the three shapes in the blank grid. The three shapes are moving around the perimeter of the grid in an anti-clockwise direction.

Q12 A
The arrow moves down the grids as the sequence progresses, alternating between the middle two columns. The pairs of black and grey dots move down and up the grids.

Q13 D

The number of sides on the shapes increase in an anti-clockwise direction around the corners of the grid. The sides increase from 3 to 4, to 5 therefore the shape in the top right should have six sides. The shapes in the corners of the diagonals are the same colour, ie the hexagon should be grey.

Q14 B

The bottom row and middle row are combined in the top row, with the bottom row being in the foreground and the middle row being in the background.

Q15 E

The top and bottom rows combine to make the middle row with the top row in the foreground and bottom row in the background.

Shuffled Sentences

Q1 A

an

Debris was strewn across the neighbourhood's streets as a result of last night's storm.

Q2 A

whether

The bad weather caused severe delays to flights at the airport.

Q3 D

those

This is likely to make a big difference.

Q4 A

tree

She decided to leaf through the book whilst in the bookshop

Q5 D

although

It was now the responsibility of the parents.

Q6 B

there

The scores were all checked to confirm their accuracy.

Q7 C

scene

She was astounded by what she had just seen.

Q8 D

mirrored

The central location was ideal for them.

Q9 A

hanging

The basket was positioned in the hallway.

Q10 B

sunk

Several attempts were made to recover the cargo.

Q11 D

taken

The journey took three hours by car.

Q12 A

kicked

The dress code stipulated formal attire for the annual charity ball.

Q13 A

waist

The chest of drawers provided extra storage in the bedroom.

Q14 D

must

Use of cameras was prohibited in the theatre.

Q15 B

accept

A discount was offered in return for payment in cash.

Answers to Test D Paper 1

Comprehension

1. C

Body language and eye movements

2. E

To further their career and to bring them success

3. C

Misunderstood

4. D

The details from the meetings can be easily sent to a significant amount of people.

5. B

The size of mobile phones has reduced and their capabilities have increased.

6. A

A large number of emails are unread or deleted.

7. B

Adjective

8. C

An item that people use in their everyday life

9. A

User-friendly

10. C

Elderly people are being taught how to communicate via social media.

Numeracy

1. D

3004

2. B

23

$144 - 121 = 23$

3. E

98

$294 \div 3 = 98$

4. D

108°

interior + exterior = 180°

exterior = 360 ÷ 5 (number of sides) = 72°

interior = 180 − 72 = 108°

5. C

4

Substitute information in the question:

$4 = 2a - 4$

so rearranged,

$8 = 2a$, and $a = 4$

6. D

1

Substitute information in the question:

$8a - 8 = 0$, so $8a = 8$, and $a = 1$

7. B

5

$15 + ? = 20$, so $? = 5$

8. B

10

$8 \times ? = 72 + 8$

$8 \times ? = 80$

$? = 10$

9. E

15

$? + 15 = 30$

$? = 15$

10. C

2

1 roll costs £1.50 × 3 = £4.50

For £10, I can buy 2 rolls costing £9 and I will have £1 left over.

11. E

1 in 6

The number the die lands on does not depend on the previous throws, and there are 6 faces which are equally likely for the die to land on.

12. A

16

$5 + 22 - 11 = 16$

13. B

5

15 would like pizza. Of the 15 pizza slices, one-third were not eaten, so 5 remain.

14. C

35

From right to left, the sequence increases by an increasing amount, with each difference being 1 higher than the last. Differences are 2, 3, 4, 5 so next is a difference of 6 (added onto 29 to give 35).

15. C

26

16. B

8

56 divided by 7 = 8

17. D

96

Headlines are shown 4 times per hour,

4×24 (hours in a day) = 96

18. A

1.6

Difference is doubling between each consecutive pair of numbers in the sequence. Next difference is 0.8.

19. B

one-fifth of 160

In order of answers: 31, 32, 31.5, 31, 31.33

20. E

9

$5 - 3 + 7 = 9$

21. D

57

Range is highest less the lowest = 81 − 24 = 57

22. A

52.5

Mean is the sum of the data, divided by the number of pieces of data = 420 ÷ 8 = 52.5

23. C

58.5

Find middle data value when arranged in size order:

24, 24, 34, 53, 64, 68, 72, 81 so halfway between 53 and 64, which is 117 ÷ 2 = 58.5

24. C

40

25. A

2006–2012

Need to find the only 2 years listed in the answers between which the % of the higher value is 5 times that of the lower.

26. E

2012–2013

27. C

32 and $\frac{1}{3}$

Divide the sum of the data by 9 (the number of pieces of data).

291 ÷ 9 = 32.333

28. D

89

One additional year means there are now 10 years. This means that as the mean is 38, the total of all 10 years data must be 10 × 38 = 380. After 9 years, the sum was 291, so the 10th year (2014) must be 380 − 291 = 89% of children.

Synonyms

1. B routinely		**11. A** hurry	
2. D distort		**12. E** amount	
3. A vitality		**13. B** devour	
4. E unfold		**14. E** civilised	
5. B remember		**15. E** happy	
6. B company		**16. B** emanate	
7. C classic		**17. C** polite	
8. E admission		**18. D** tranquil	
9. B spirited		**19. B** lessen	
10. D gratitude		**20. C** series	

Non-Verbal Reasoning

1. B

This is a half turn of the original image.

2. D

This is a quarter turn anticlockwise of the original image.

3. C

The only answer where closing the shapes together does not make a hexagon.

4. B

The only answer where the rectangle and the shape it leads into are not the same shade. (There is shading on one of the triangles, but not on the rectangle.)

5. B

The only answer where the rectangles do not join at the ends – one joins another rectangle in the middle.

6. B

The only answer where there are not black, grey and white shapes.

7. E

The only answer where closing the shapes together makes a 3-sided shape, rather than a quadrilateral. E is also the only image made up of different-sized shapes.

8. E

The only answer where there is not a white shape inside.

9. A

The only answer where there is not a grey triangle in the background.

10. B

The only answer where the arrow does not point to the left.

11. D

The only answer where the stem is in background, and flower in foreground.

12. B

The only answer where the arrow is rotating anticlockwise.

13. B

14. C

15. D

Answers to Test D Paper 2

Cloze Sentences

1. **F**
   The blood was **extracted** from the ancient specimen.
2. **G**
   The judge's **ruling** was final.
3. **E**
   The **subterranean** cave was dark and cold.
4. **I**
   The parking signs gave the residents **ample** warning that the road would close at midnight.
5. **C**
   The work was painstaking and **laborious.**
6. **D**
   The animal's limb was **fractured** in several places.
7. **J**
   The journey came to an end and the **adventure** was over.
8. **A**
   The film was a **fantastical** story, set in space.
9. **H**
   The athlete's dedication to her training had set a high **standard.**
10. **B**
    After a day of walking in the mountains, the boy felt **dehydrated.**
11. **rim**
    The hairdresser **trim**med the girl's hair.
12. **cap**
    The lands**cap**e was rugged.
13. **son**
    The project failed for one rea**son**.
14. **bat**
    The boy **bat**hed in the glorious sunshine.
15. **oil**
    The girl's clothes were sp**oil**ed when she splashed in the mud.
16. **are**
    Does this car have a sp**are** tyre?
17. **pin**
    The s**pin**e of the book had broken and all the pages had fallen out.

Problem Solving

1. **C**
   8
   $\frac{3}{4}$ of 12 = 9, 9 − 2 = 7, plus Edward equals 8
2. **D**
   10
   $\left(\frac{3}{4}\ of\ 12 + 1\right)$
3. **H**
   £84
   10 + 2 = 12 × 7 = £84
4. **I**
   £94
5. **B**
   £104
   (8.50 × 10) + (9.50 × 2)
6. **E**
   1 hour and 35 minutes = 95 minutes
7. **G**
   85
   68 + 12 − 13 + 18 = 85
8. **F**
   7
   85 from previous question less 78 = 7
9. **A**
   35
10. **J**
    4
    1 km in 15 minutes is the same as walking at 4 km/h as 1 hour is 60 minutes, and in 60 minutes they would cover 4 km.

Antonyms

1. **B** uninformed
2. **D** logical
3. **D** infant
4. **E** hairy
5. **B** tradesman
6. **A** nourish
7. **A** dull
8. **D** planned
9. **B** vacate
10. **C** tired
11. **E** expand
12. **A** profit
13. **B** plain
14. **C** main
15. **D** level
16. **B** rumour
17. **C** dilute
18. **A** aggravate

19. **D** *colossal*
20. **E** *assemble*
21. **B** *imbalanced*
22. **D** *animosity*
23. **B** *opening*
24. **C** *follower*
25. **D** *exciting*

Non-Verbal Reasoning

1. **C**
   Net requires half-turn rotation, use the cross that will then be on top.
2. **D**
   No rotation of net required.
3. **B**
   No rotation of net required.
4. **A**
   Net requires half-turn rotation.
5. **D**
   Net requires half-turn rotation.
6. **E**
   CD The first letter relates to the shading. The second letter relates to the shape.
7. **C**
   BE The first letter relates to the position of the arrows. The second letter relates to the position of the star.
8. **A**
   YS The first letter relates to the shape in the foreground. The second letter relates to the number of shapes.
9. **C**
   HC The first letter relates to the shape in the foreground. The second letter relates to whether the arrow crosses the shapes.
10. **A**
    TS The first letter relates to the position of the $\frac{3}{4}$ circle. The second letter relates to whether the trapezium overlaps the $\frac{3}{4}$ circle.
11. **D**
    UG The first letter relates to the shading of the shape. The second letter relates to the position of the shape. The arrows are irrelevant.
12. **E**
    Reflection in a horizontal line.
13. **D**
    Reflection in a vertical line.
14. **B**
    Reflection in a horizontal line.
15. **D**
    Reflection in a diagonal line to the top right or bottom left of the image.

Shuffled Sentences

1. **A**
   shelled
   We live in a small but beautiful house overlooking the sea.
2. **B**
   chimney
   The stars twinkled in the moonlit sky and the air was misty.
3. **E**
   noisy
   The advert stated unbeatable discounts but the shop was overpriced.
4. **C**
   candidly
   The van was parked at the entrance of the site.
5. **A**
   digger
   The ancient subterranean mine was dug by hand.
6. **B**
   tears
   The sight of the sunrise stirred my emotions.
7. **C**
   achievement
   The boy achieved full marks in his times tables test.
   The words 'to' and 'went' do not appear in the shuffled sentence and can be eliminated immediately.
8. **D**
   enforced
   The tunnel was stabilised with steel.
9. **A**
   there
   High unemployment is a problem in many countries.

10. *E*
packet
The diamond shone in the dazzling sunlight.

11. *C*
landed
As he collected his son from school he noticed that his bag was missing.

12. *E*
elongated
You have to listen carefully to the people talking to answer the questions.

13. *D*
rounded
He placed the evidence in a bag.

14. *B*
view
Let's go for a run up the hill.

15. *E*
looked
Look at this strange looking plant.

Pupil's Full Name:

Instructions:
Mark the boxes correctly like this ⊟

Please sign your name here:

Comprehension

Example 1

⊟ᴬ ᴮ ᶜ ᴰ ᴱ

Practice Question 1

ᴬ ᴮ ᶜ ᴰ ᴱ

	A	B	C	D	E
1	A	B	C	D	E
2	A	B	C	D	E
3	A	B	C	D	E
4	A	B	C	D	E
5	A	B	C	D	E
6	A	B	C	D	E
7	A	B	C	D	E
8	A	B	C	D	E
9	A	B	C	D	E
10	A	B	C	D	E

Grammar

Example 1

ᴬ ᴮ ᶜ ᴰ ⊟ᴱ

Practice Question 1

ᴬ ᴮ ᶜ ᴰ ᴱ

	A	B	C	D	E
1	A	B	C	D	E
2	A	B	C	D	E
3	A	B	C	D	E
4	A	B	C	D	E
5	A	B	C	D	E
6	A	B	C	D	E
7	A	B	C	D	E
8	A	B	C	D	E
9	A	B	C	D	E

Numeracy

Example 1

ᴬ ᴮ ᶜ ᴰ ⊟ᴱ

Practice Question 1

ᴬ ᴮ ᶜ ᴰ ᴱ

	A	B	C	D	E
1	A	B	C	D	E
2	A	B	C	D	E
3	A	B	C	D	E
4	A	B	C	D	E
5	A	B	C	D	E
6	A	B	C	D	E
7	A	B	C	D	E
8	A	B	C	D	E
9	A	B	C	D	E
10	A	B	C	D	E
11	A	B	C	D	E
12	A	B	C	D	E
13	A	B	C	D	E
14	A	B	C	D	E
15	A	B	C	D	E
16	A	B	C	D	E
17	A	B	C	D	E
18	A	B	C	D	E
19	A	B	C	D	E
20	A	B	C	D	E
21	A	B	C	D	E
22	A	B	C	D	E
23	A	B	C	D	E
24	A	B	C	D	E
25	A	B	C	D	E
26	A	B	C	D	E
27	A	B	C	D	E
28	A	B	C	D	E
29	A	B	C	D	E
30	A	B	C	D	E
31	A	B	C	D	E
32	A	B	C	D	E

	A	B	C	D	E
33	A	B	C	D	E
34	A	B	C	D	E
35	A	B	C	D	E
36	A	B	C	D	E
37	A	B	C	D	E
38	A	B	C	D	E
39	A	B	C	D	E

Synonyms

Example 1

A   B   C   D   E

Practice Question 1

	A	B	C	D	E
1	A	B	C	D	E
2	A	B	C	D	E
3	A	B	C	D	E
4	A	B	C	D	E
5	A	B	C	D	E
6	A	B	C	D	E
7	A	B	C	D	E
8	A	B	C	D	E
9	A	B	C	D	E
10	A	B	C	D	E
11	A	B	C	D	E
12	A	B	C	D	E
13	A	B	C	D	E
14	A	B	C	D	E
15	A	B	C	D	E
16	A	B	C	D	E
17	A	B	C	D	E
18	A	B	C	D	E
19	A	B	C	D	E
20	A	B	C	D	E

Non-Verbal Reasoning

COMPLETE THE SEQUENCE
Example 1

A   B   C   D   E

COMPLETE THE SEQUENCE
Practice Question 1

A   B   C   D   E

ROTATION Example 2

A   B   C   D   E

ROTATION Practice Question 2

	A	B	C	D	E
1	A	B	C	D	E
2	A	B	C	D	E
3	A	B	C	D	E
4	A	B	C	D	E
5	A	B	C	D	E
6	A	B	C	D	E
7	A	B	C	D	E
8	A	B	C	D	E
9	A	B	C	D	E

Pupil's Full Name:

2

Instructions:
Mark the boxes correctly like this ⬛

Please sign your name here:

Cloze Sentences

Example 1

A   B   C   ⬛D   E

Practice Question 1

A   B   C   D   E

Example 2 _____ *ten*

Practice Question 2 _____

1	A	B	C	D	E
2	A	B	C	D	E
3	A	B	C	D	E
4	A	B	C	D	E
5	A	B	C	D	E
6	A	B	C	D	E
7	A	B	C	D	E
8	A	B	C	D	E
9	A	B	C	D	E
10	A	B	C	D	E
11	_____
12	_____
13	_____
14	_____
15	_____
16	_____
17	_____

Problem Solving

Example 1

⬛A B C D E F G H I J

Practice Question 1

A B C D E F G H I J

1	A	B	C	D	E	F	G	H	I	J
2	A	B	C	D	E	F	G	H	I	J
3	A	B	C	D	E	F	G	H	I	J
4	A	B	C	D	E	F	G	H	I	J
5	A	B	C	D	E	F	G	H	I	J
6	A	B	C	D	E	F	G	H	I	J
7	A	B	C	D	E	F	G	H	I	J
8	A	B	C	D	E	F	G	H	I	J
9	A	B	C	D	E	F	G	H	I	J
10	A	B	C	D	E	F	G	H	I	J

Antonyms

Example 1

~~A~~   B   C   D   E

Practice Question 1

A   B   C   D   E

1   A   B   C   D   E
2   A   B   C   D   E
3   A   B   C   D   E
4   A   B   C   D   E
5   A   B   C   D   E
6   A   B   C   D   E
7   A   B   C   D   E
8   A   B   C   D   E
9   A   B   C   D   E
10   A   B   C   D   E
11   A   B   C   D   E
12   A   B   C   D   E
13   A   B   C   D   E
14   A   B   C   D   E
15   A   B   C   D   E
16   A   B   C   D   E
17   A   B   C   D   E
18   A   B   C   D   E
19   A   B   C   D   E
20   A   B   C   D   E
21   A   B   C   D   E
22   A   B   C   D   E
23   A   B   C   D   E
24   A   B   C   D   E
25   A   B   C   D   E

Non – Verbal Reasoning

CODES Example 1

A   B   C   D   ~~E~~

CODES Practice Question 1

A   B   C   D   E

COMPLETE THE SQUARE Example 2

A   B   C   ~~D~~   E

**COMPLETE THE SQUARE
Practice Question 2**

A   B   C   D   E

1   A   B   C   D   E
2   A   B   C   D   E

3   A   B   C   D   E
4   A   B   C   D   E
5   A   B   C   D   E
6   A   B   C   D   E
7   A   B   C   D   E
8   A   B   C   D   E
9   A   B   C   D   E
10   A   B   C   D   E
11   A   B   C   D   E
12   A   B   C   D   E
13   A   B   C   D   E
14   A   B   C   D   E
15   A   B   C   D   E

Shuffled Sentences

Example 1

~~A~~   B   C   D   E

Practice Questions 1

A   B   C   D   E

1   A   B   C   D   E
2   A   B   C   D   E
3   A   B   C   D   E
4   A   B   C   D   E
5   A   B   C   D   E
6   A   B   C   D   E
7   A   B   C   D   E
8   A   B   C   D   E
9   A   B   C   D   E
10   A   B   C   D   E
11   A   B   C   D   E
12   A   B   C   D   E
13   A   B   C   D   E
14   A   B   C   D   E
15   A   B   C   D   E

Pupil's Full Name:

Instructions:
Mark the boxes correctly like this ▬

Please sign your name here:

Comprehension

Example 1

A̶ B C D E

Practice Question 1

A B C D E

1	A	B	C	D	E
2	A	B	C	D	E
3	A	B	C	D	E
4	A	B	C	D	E
5	A	B	C	D	E
6	A	B	C	D	E
7	A	B	C	D	E
8	A	B	C	D	E
9	A	B	C	D	E
10	A	B	C	D	E

Numeracy

Example 1

A B C D E̶

Practice Question 1

A B C D E

1	A	B	C	D	E
2	A	B	C	D	E
3	A	B	C	D	E
4	A	B	C	D	E
5	A	B	C	D	E
6	A	B	C	D	E
7	A	B	C	D	E
8	A	B	C	D	E
9	A	B	C	D	E
10	A	B	C	D	E

11	A	B	C	D	E
12	A	B	C	D	E
13	A	B	C	D	E
14	A	B	C	D	E
15	A	B	C	D	E
16	A	B	C	D	E
17	A	B	C	D	E
18	A	B	C	D	E
19	A	B	C	D	E
20	A	B	C	D	E
21	A	B	C	D	E
22	A	B	C	D	E
23	A	B	C	D	E
24	A	B	C	D	E
25	A	B	C	D	E
26	A	B	C	D	E
27	A	B	C	D	E
28	A	B	C	D	E

Synonyms

Example 1

    A   B   C   D   E̶

Practice Question 1

    A   B   C   D   E

#	A	B	C	D	E
1	A	B	C	D	E
2	A	B	C	D	E
3	A	B	C	D	E
4	A	B	C	D	E
5	A	B	C	D	E
6	A	B	C	D	E
7	A	B	C	D	E
8	A	B	C	D	E
9	A	B	C	D	E
10	A	B	C	D	E
11	A	B	C	D	E
12	A	B	C	D	E
13	A	B	C	D	E
14	A	B	C	D	E
15	A	B	C	D	E
16	A	B	C	D	E
17	A	B	C	D	E
18	A	B	C	D	E
19	A	B	C	D	E
20	A	B	C	D	E

Non-Verbal Reasoning

REFLECTION Example 1

    A   B   C   D   E̶

REFLECTION Practice Question 1

    A   B   C   D   E

ROTATION Example 2

    A   B   C̶   D   E

ROTATION Practice Question 2

    A   B   C   D   E

LEAST SIMILAR Example 3

    A   B̶   C   D   E

LEAST SIMILAR Practice Question 3

    A   B   C   D   E

#	A	B	C	D	E
1	A	B	C	D	E
2	A	B	C	D	E
3	A	B	C	D	E
4	A	B	C	D	E
5	A	B	C	D	E
6	A	B	C	D	E
7	A	B	C	D	E
8	A	B	C	D	E
9	A	B	C	D	E
10	A	B	C	D	E
11	A	B	C	D	E
12	A	B	C	D	E
13	A	B	C	D	E
14	A	B	C	D	E
15	A	B	C	D	E

Synonyms

Example 1

Practice Question 1

Pupil's Full Name:

Instructions:
Mark the boxes correctly like this ▅

Please sign your name here:

Cloze Sentences

Example 1

⊼ B C D E F G H I J

Practice Question 1

A B C D E F G H I J

Example 2 _____ ten

Practice Question 2 _____

1 A B C D E F G H I J
2 A B C D E F G H I J
3 A B C D E F G H I J
4 A B C D E F G H I J
5 A B C D E F G H I J
6 A B C D E F G H I J
7 A B C D E F G H I J
8 A B C D E F G H I J
9 A B C D E F G H I J
10 A B C D E F G H I J
11 _____
12 _____
13 _____
14 _____
15 _____
16 _____
17 _____

Problem Solving

Example 1

⊼ B C D E F G H I J

Practice Question 1

A B C D E F G H I J

1 A B C D E F G H I J
2 A B C D E F G H I J
3 A B C D E F G H I J
4 A B C D E F G H I J
5 A B C D E F G H I J
6 A B C D E F G H I J
7 A B C D E F G H I J
8 A B C D E F G H I J
9 A B C D E F G H I J
10 A B C D E F G H I J

Antonyms

Example 1

    A   B   C   D   E

Practice Question 1

    A   B   C   D   E

1. A B C D E
2. A B C D E
3. A B C D E
4. A B C D E
5. A B C D E
6. A B C D E
7. A B C D E
8. A B C D E
9. A B C D E
10. A B C D E
11. A B C D E
12. A B C D E
13. A B C D E
14. A B C D E
15. A B C D E
16. A B C D E
17. A B C D E
18. A B C D E
19. A B C D E
20. A B C D E
21. A B C D E
22. A B C D E
23. A B C D E
24. A B C D E
25. A B C D E

Non – Verbal Reasoning

CUBES Example 1

    A   B   C   D   E

CUBES Practice Question 1

    A   B   C   D   E

REFLECTION Example 2

    A   B   C   D   E

REFLECTION Practice Question 2

    A   B   C   D   E

1. A B C D E
2. A B C D E
3. A B C D E

4. A B C D E
5. A B C D E
6. A B C D E
7. A B C D E
8. A B C D E
9. A B C D E
10. A B C D E
11. A B C D E
12. A B C D E
13. A B C D E
14. A B C D E
15. A B C D E

Shuffled Sentences

Example 1

    A   B   C   D   E

Practice Questions 1

    A   B   C   D   E

1. A B C D E
2. A B C D E
3. A B C D E
4. A B C D E
5. A B C D E
6. A B C D E
7. A B C D E
8. A B C D E
9. A B C D E
10. A B C D E
11. A B C D E
12. A B C D E
13. A B C D E
14. A B C D E
15. A B C D E